LETTERS TO DANIEL

LETTERS
TO DANIEL

SERGIO BAMBARÉN

For Daniel,

With Love and Light...

Your father, Sergio

Life is short...
Forgive quickly,
Kiss slowly,
Love truly,
Laugh uncontrollably...
And never regret anything
That made you smile,
Or cry.

PROLOGUE

The last three years of my life have been devoted almost exclusively to make a dream come true: to produce a full-length animation movie based on my first novel, "The Dolphin: The Story of a Dreamer."

But during the process of developing the film, something even more important happened: life gave me the most beautiful treasure a man can ask for – a son.

I always say it: life works in strange, but wonderful ways. At the beginning it was a phone call from three great German friends, Lillian, Thomas and Joachim, all experts in the world of films and documentaries. Through my literary agent, they bought the option to make a film of the first short novel I wrote more than ten years ago. Of course I accepted. Who knows, maybe the dream of turning the book into a film could come true.

At the same time, I was already thinking about going back to my roots, to the country where I was born, where the animation industry had recently started to flourish. So I rented an apartment that had a beautiful view of the ocean, with dolphins in my sight almost daily, sleeping at night with the music of the crashing surf. It was ten blocks from the house I was born in, so long ago, the perfect place where I could put on paper what my soul whispered to my heart. I also fell in love with a beautiful woman, Deborah.

Anyway, after settling in my birthplace city with Deborah, I started to discover what the local industry was doing in animation, and I was truly inspired by the creativity of my countrymen, There was only one thing missing: giving these artists the tools and the state-of-the-art hardware and software available in the studios of developed countries.

So one day an animation director I knew called me, and we spoke for two hours. I wrote down some figures and found some investors interested in the project. We surrounded ourselves with the best people we could find – not only artists, but also wonderful human beings – and we decided to go ahead with the project, starting with the material my German friends had already created. We made them our associate partners, and started working with fifty state of the art computers, compared to the three or four thousand computers that the big studios normally work with.

David and Goliath…

Why not?

And the voice of my heart was whispering me what I once heard in a beautiful movie called "Field of Dreams," with Kevin Costner as the protagonist: "If you build it, they will come..."

Throughout the good and bad times I kept telling all my colleagues: make your best effort, love what you do, use your passion…the rest will follow naturally.

I put only one condition to the "Dreamer's Club," as we called ourselves. My only involvement, I told them, was to ensure that the message and the soul of the book would appear clearly in the film. Let's make a movie that will help people remember their dreams, and remind them that the most important things in life are invisible to the eye.

But life had other plans for me, and without even asking for it, I ended being the producer of the film...

But as I said at the beginning, another amazing experience happened in my life:

I had a son!

The first day I heard the news from Deborah that she was pregnant, I was in shock. The next day I was speechless. But when I woke up in the morning of the third day, I was a very happy, very peaceful man.

Now I know that I can live this wonderful world with no regrets, no hard feelings at all. What this small and wonderful creature has done to my heart is indescribable. He gazes at me, and it seems like I am gazing at myself. He wakes up every day with a smile, no matter what, and once in a while he puts his little hands and his face on the glass of the balcony, staring at the ocean for hours.

He is the reason for this story and this book – the story of parts of my life, and how I, a simple and common human being learned so many important things in my journey by choosing to walk the road less traveled.

As a boy, my mother used to leave small slivers of paper on my bed containing heartfelt thoughts that had come to her. I'd read them in the just after I woke. I learned so much about life through her heart and her eyes!

I will try my best to do the same with you, my beloved Daniel. It's a promise.

Letters to Daniel
...and how I built my happiness,
Here, on Earth...

Hi, Daniel

This is Sergio, the man that they call your father. Well, at least in the society we live in.

The way I see it Daniel, is that I am the human being that planted the seed of life in the womb of your beautiful mother. But I can only talk about myself, and let others live their lives the way they want. Having said that, I will always be Sergio for you, if that's what you want. But if you want me to call me father, that's fine, too.

Daniel, you must know that I was one of those human beings that never thought about having children. I thought it wasn't in my genes. Funny, however, that as the years went by and life gave me so many gifts without asking anything in return, I suddenly started to see these small human beings running all around me, and something in my heart changed dramatically. I started to feel a special bond with them: maybe because of their innocence, maybe because I was amazed that they were so happy with the simple things of life: living life as an adventure each day, never worrying about what the future would bring, just enjoying the moment as if there was no tomorrow: living one day at a time: just as you do, Daniel.

Yes, my beloved Daniel. I am still amazed that you are surrounded with all kind of fancy toys, and fashionable clothes: everything a grown-up would desire. Yet your favorite toy is an empty bottle of Johnson and Johnson's baby shampoo. You could live without all the toys that inundate your room. But don't let one even try to take *away your empty baby shampoo bottle! It's your most cherished treasure! Just like Oskar, your pet Scottish terrier who has gradually become one of your best friends. Some years ago, Daniel, as I was sitting in the beach watching the ocean, I grabbed a beautiful pebble, and took it home. I gave it to Oskar to play with it, and from that day on, he forgot about his plastic bones and all other toys we had given him: it's the only thing that Oskar keeps in his little wooden house where he sleeps. His most cherished treasure. Just like your empty shampoo bottle.*

Yes, Daniel. Maybe you still don't know it, although by the way you look at me, sometimes I think you do. I guess you are one of the most beautiful treasures life has given me, not because you always wake up with a smile in your face, the same way I did when I was your age; not only because now that you are starting to walk you want to discover everything that surrounds you. You are so curious! The same way I was when I was your age.

I guess it is because you've made me remember, deep in my heart, the child that I once was, and always will be, no matter how old I am. You've brought me back to my roots, Daniel: to the kid that used to sit in the in the border of the high cliffs of the place I was born, aged five, just staring at the ocean and the waves, the seagulls and the dolphins, and playing with the clouds as the sun set in the horizon, turning the sky into a palette of wonderful colors; for at that age the word fear hadn't been planted in my mind.

So, these letters that come from the bottom of my heart are for you, Daniel: from a grown-up child to a boy who is just starting to wonder at the world. It is a small gift written with so much love. The kind of love I had never experienced before: a love so pure and unique that I believe it would be an offense to try to explain it in words.

In these pages I will tell you stories I have never told anyone, because I know you won't judge me. In some small way, perhaps, the life I have lived and still live will help you always remember where you come from, Daniel, and help you remember why you came to this world. Because sooner or later, life and the society you live in will complicate things for you and sometimes make you feel lost: When you feel that way, I hope you will come to me and we will talk, young child to old child, and maybe I can help you clear your mind, as well as mine. And when my time has come to leave this world, I hope these words written forever in paper will help you always realize that this journey called life, with all its good and bad experiences, is a wonderful adventure, if you live it the way I have live it: listening to the voice of your heart, building your own trail instead of following somebody else's, and one day at a time. The only things that truly belong to you, Daniel, are your dreams and the free will to live your life the way you want to live it. Everything else in this life is only borrowed; probably the most important lesson I've learnt so far, and a key ingredient on the journey to happiness, the way I see it. I also hope that these words will help you understand who I am, deep inside, and why I have lived my life the way I have.

But let's leave it there, OK? There are many things I want to share with you... until that unique day when you will be able to fly with your own wings and nobody else's.

Just one last thing, Daniel:

Never forget that the love I feel for you is like the wind:
I cannot see it, but I can always feel it, no matter where you are, or where I am.

With all my love,
Sergio

In the arms of my beloved mother. I was 2 years old.

I

I was born to a middle class family in the Clínica Americana, the private hospital where my father was the head of the psychiatry department. I clearly remember the day I was born, and of course, many people have told me throughout my life that it's impossible to have such a memory, that I was inventing the story. But over the years I have learned that the word impossible only exists in the minds of those who permit that words such as impossible, envy, hate, resentment, greediness and others exist in their mind. Talking just about myself, it's as easy as reading a dictionary: I close my eyes, and in the dictionary that dwells in my mind and in my heart, with time and practice I have been able to erase most of these words that are a obstacles in the journey to true happiness.

How I do remember? Well, for those that still tell me it's impossible to remember the moment you arrive in this world, my father and my pediatrician, both present at the moment I was born, told me that after cleaning me and soothing me before tucking me in a little hospital blanket, I opened my eyes, yawned and stared at them with open eyes. They were amazed. And after the initial moments of shock, being taken from a warm floating salty space where I fell so safe, I stopped crying. I opened my eyes once again, saw this wonderful face (that I now know was my mother's face), staring at me with such indescribable love in her eyes that I stared back at her and smiled. And then I fell asleep, knowing that I had only been moved from one wonderful place to another: from the warm womb of my mother to her tender embrace. I smiled once again, knowing everything would be okay. That's all I remember.

As I was saying, I was born into a middle-class family that owned an old big house that overlooked the cliffs on which the Miraflores district in the Lima, Peru is located. Fifty-meter high cliffs overlook the ocean and the vast horizon. I slept in a small room on the second floor that had a French window and a small porch where I could go out and smell the breeze of the ocean and watch the crashing surf below the cliffs. Once in a while a seagull would come to the porch to say hello.

That is how my relationship with the world and with nature started, surrounded by the ocean and the seagulls, a caring father, an older brother, and a wonderful mother. From her I inherited most of the good things I am blessed to carry in my genes: her sensibility, her love of life and the simple things that make life a wonderful journey, and her big heart. But nothing is perfect, and in time I would find that I had also inherited from her a medical problem that I now know I can live with, thanks to the development of third-generation medicines: depression.

From my father, and I say this with humility, I inherited a sense of empathy and his questioning approach toward the world. My father has a very special relationship with his patients, and I can say he is a real doctor, always caring about them, charging for his services to those who can pay, and not charging a cent to those who can't. He was born to be a doctor, and much more. I have seen the love in the faces of his patients: he really connects with them, making them feel better, not only physically, but also spiritually. No matter the time, day or the middle of the night, if a patient called for help my father would always get dressed and drive to the clinic or the patient's house to help him the way he only knew. He was a man of principles, something I will always thank him for teaching me. However, again, nothing is perfect, and I inherited from him a weakness for alcohol: luckily, for both of us, we were both able to overcome this terrible disease long ago. We accepted that we were basically "allergic" to alcohol and kept it out of our lives.

So that is how I arrived at this world: with a great father, a loving mother, and a brother one year older than me, with whom I would fight day and night, as brothers do, but who would be always be there to defend me if somebody else tried to harm me. He would always defend me, always.

I didn't have the luck to know my grandparents – just one of them, my father's father, a very wise psychiatrist who had a lovely smile for all of his grandchildren. He was the man who gave me my first job, when I was seven years old. He also taught me that hard work is not only is a decent way of making a living, but also keeps your body and mind in a healthy state.

I thought life would always stay that simple. Yet I never realized how things could sometimes change from one day to the other, and how people change with time.

But as long as I had my view of the endless ocean and I could talk with the seagulls, I was a happy child.

Daniel and I

Hi, Daniel

It feels like yesterday the day you were born. How time flies!

It was a truly amazing experience to see you entering this world Daniel. Luckily, everything went well with your birth. But I noticed something when you took your first breath and started to cry. I felt that you were crying not because "that it is the way is has to be" but because you were removed from a lovely and safe place that you called home for the last nine months: the warm and tender womb of your mother, floating in salty water, feeling the peace and tranquility of a space where no harm had yet been done to your heart and your soul. I felt a little sad for you. Maybe you wanted to stay inside for another nine months, just in case, to be better prepared for the world you were about to enter. But Nature is wise, and things must happen when they must.

I see you now, almost a year later, and you are already walking. You want to explore everything! And sometimes you get so excited, that with your still fragile walk you stumble and fall. Everyone tells me that we should avoid letting you fall, but I always say the same: "Let him fall". And as any grown-up knows, when you stumble what worries you the most Daniel, is not the stumbling itself, but if somebody is watching you. But if you fall and we don't watch you Daniel, you don't cry. With your little wonderful tiny hands you struggle to stand up again, and you always stand up again. And a smile illuminates your face.

I admire watching you do that, Daniel: falling but getting up again, all by yourself; because those small steps that you are starting to take would seem irrelevant to others, but not for you. Tough times will come in the future, Daniel, when you will stumble in life and maybe feel lost. But as long as you keep that wonderful smile with which you wake up every morning and not feel ashamed to stumble and make mistakes and learn the lesson, you will live the life you came to live, free of prejudices and not paying attention to what others might say or think.

I know you will. It's in your genes, in your dark eyes, and in your heart!

Your father,

Sergio.

II

I had a wonderful childhood. Not only at home, but also with the friends I made in my neighborhood and at school. I was lucky to attend a British School, Markham College, a school that in those days was considered second to none – and still is.

I still remember the first day that my mother took me to kindergarten, wearing an apron. Suddenly I saw myself surrounded by many kids who, like me, were holding to their mother's hand. And I remember many of them were crying. For some mothers, leaving their kids in the classroom with Miss Martin, a lovely young Australian lady, was a traumatic experience. Screaming children would beg their mother not to leave them there. But as time passed by, most mothers started to walk away, others hidden behind the French windows of the class, staring at their loved ones, proud to see them in a safe place where they would learn many important things about life.

In my case, I was so amazed with the new environment that I didn't realize when my mother had left me. She was hiding outside the classroom, watching me carefully, and she thought I couldn't see her. But I was truly focused on a wonderful pin that my teacher Miss Martin had on her blouse, glowing like a golden treasure. She noticed my interest, and came to me. She gave me a kiss, took the pin carefully off her blouse and pinned it on my apron.

"This is for you" she said, smiling. Then she gave me another kiss and on went back to the front of the class.

We were about to experience our first "lesson", and truly it was beautiful. In order to break the tension, she put some music in an old music player, and said, "let's dance!" In no time, we were all dancing, if you can call that dancing! I would say we were all jumping up and down, starting to know each other by just moving around in our new surroundings

But as I was jumping up and down like the rest, I couldn't stop staring at the golden pin that Miss Martin had placed on my uniform. Later when my mother picked me up I would learn that the pin depicted a kangaroo, an animal I had never seen before.

A kind of premonition of things to come?

I didn't know it at that time. But 40 years later I now know that indeed it was a sign of things to come; but only if I followed the dictates of my heart and decided to live the live I had chosen to live: following my dreams, taking tough decisions at some critical times in my life; not listening to the voice of the crowds, but only listening to the voice of my heart.

Dear Daniel,

Yesterday was the first day I picked you up from the pre-kindergarten you are starting to make friends and discover the world, surrounded by wonderful teachers who love small children.

I have to tell you I felt a little frightened. Nobody is born knowing how to be a father or a mother. You learn by trial and error. You see, when you are a kid you think that parents and your teachers have all the answers, and you feel safe when you are with them. Nothing further from the truth Daniel: grown-ups get more and more confused as they grow older.

But there is one thing that I can tell you for sure: going to school, making many friends that will probably last for a lifetime. Playing with other kids and having fun are some of the memories you will most treasure throughout your whole life, Daniel.

I know that sometimes you will get tired or too lazy to do your homework, maybe you will get into a fight with another kid. Sometimes you will try to trick us, by saying: "I feel sick" and maybe you won't go to school that day. I used the trick of placing a banana skin in my armpit the night before. It always worked! Next morning I would wake up with high fever... until one day my father, as the good doctor he was, discovered my trick. So no more bananas at home!

But one thing I can guarantee you, Daniel: the friends you make in school will be all your life around you; because after spending so much time together, day after day, week after week, year after year, you will learn to know each other so well that your memories with them will last for a lifetime. For when you grow up and the world gets complicated, gathering with your friends from school will be a wonderful moment to remember your wonder years of the past: kind of a stress relief.

So enjoy your wonder years of childhood, Daniel; try not to be mean with other children; sometimes, without knowing it, you leave scars in those children that will take them many years to overcome. And I don't mean physical scars, but spiritual ones, the ones that hurt the most and last much longer.

Believe me Daniel: I would give everything I have just to go back to my childhood and spent just one single day with my friends at school again.

Enjoy your wonder years, Daniel, you will cherish them forever.

With love,

Sergio

III

I was very lucky that most of my best friends from school lived near my home. Getting together was no problem. Just hanging around together, listening to the radio, and growing up safely. We'd all climb to a wonderful tree full of branches where we could sit and talk, read magazines, and enjoy each other's company. Our school was a boy's-only school, and its sister school, called San Silvestre, also a British School, was where most of the sisters of my best friends studied. This would prove fantastic as the years went by, for when we started growing up we would become a group of around twenty boys and girls that would go together everywhere: the best group of friends I have ever had Daniel, and probably will.

With the girls we would discover what summer love was: the naïveté of staring at the girl you liked, and when she turned to see you, you would immediately turn somewhere else. That kind of innocent love that makes you feel nervous, and even keep you awake all night. "Will she feel the same way I feel for her?"

During those years of growing up, and living so close to the ocean, one day we decided to explore the beaches that lay below the high cliffs of the city. In those times a dirt trail would be the only way to descend to the shore, trails only used by tanned fishermen who eked out a living from the sea. It was the 60's, and you could walk along the pebble-covered shores, and watch the crashing surf.

But besides the odd fisherman, they were these crazy guys, not too many of them, sitting on a long, wooden board on the ocean, where the waves were breaking. Suddenly one of them would turn his wooden board toward the shore and start paddling hard until his board caught the same speed of the wave he was trying to catch. And when he felt that the board was moving with the wave, he would immediately stand up in his board, turn it sideways and start gliding through the wall of water that was about to break. I was spellbound: it looked so natural, so free, so right...

And that day, not only I, but also my faithful friends, made a promise: that we would work hard after school to make enough money to buy what at that time was known as a Hawaiian surfboard.

My beloved Daniel,

Being young is not a period of your life.

Being young is more of a state of mind. It has nothing to do with growing old or not having wrinkles in your face, Daniel; it is a matter of the will, a quality of the imagination, vigor of the emotions; it is the freshness of the deep love for life.

Youth means being able to hold to your dreams and aspirations as the years pass by, instead of starting to let your dreams fade away and hiding yourself in the safe-box. It is never quitting your yearn for excitement and replacing it for the love of ease. And this will inevitably happen as you grow older. I have known men aged sixty that feel and look younger than boys aged twenty.

You don't grow older by the amount of years you've lived, dear Daniel. You grow older when you start forgetting your dreams.

Years may wrinkle the skin, just like mine Daniel. But as long as you don't let the wrinkles touch your soul, you will always feel alive. So beware of fear, anger, resentment or hate. These are the personal enemies that will turn down your energies and will try to destroy the joy of life.

In my case Daniel, it was my endless love of the ocean and my spirit of walking that extra mile that kept me young. Walking along the road less traveled made all the difference, dear Daniel. Living my

31

life to the fullest, but not in a rush; stopping once in a while to smell the roses, and never quitting on my dreams. And always listening to the voice of your heart: your friend for life.

Can I tell you a secret Daniel? It's not the number of years you live; it has more to do with the quality of your time: stopping once in a while to stare at a sunset or a hummingbird, instead of driving day after day from the office to home, just staring at the concrete road in front of you; breaking the rules once in a while, instead of filling your brain with fears that only exist in your mind.

So Daniel, sooner or later you will have to decide. To live the live you always wanted to live, a path that sometimes can feel very lonely; or just stick to the multitudes, where the numbers will make you feel safe, but only for a while; because sooner or later, every human being will have to wake up one day and look at himself in the mirror of his own soul, and believe me, that day will be the happiest or saddest day of his life.

You were born with free will Daniel, so never forget it. I decided to live my life based in my dreams, and I never looked back: never.

Try always to discover the world with your own eyes, Daniel, and never through the eyes of others.

With true love,

Dad

IV

I learnt, thanks to my parents, and through my own experience, to live my life based on principles, and not on traditions.

Looking back now, I feel blessed to have had parents that taught me most of the principles I still base my life on: to live within your financial means, always try to do the right thing; if you make a mistake, be humble enough to accept it, learn the lesson, apologize if you have to, and move ahead. If you earn one hundred, live like you earn eighty, and to the eyes of others, live as if you earned fifty. If you have a problem that can be solved with money, then you don't have a problem. Never forget that being healthy and living in spiritual peace will always be your most important assets.

But one of the things I am most thankful for is that, since I was a child, they taught me the value of things, and the effort you had to make if you wanted to achieve something. So this brings me back to my biggest dream at that time: to purchase a Hawaiian surfboard. My father would have no problem in buying me the best surfboard you could find in the market. But instead of that he offered me a deal: "I will get you a job in which you will have to work after school. Save the money you make, and I will make up the difference and we will go together to buy the surfboard of your dreams."

Many years have passed since I made that "secret" pact with my father. We didn't tell anything to my mom: she would have freaked out, thinking about the risks of diving into rough oceans, sometimes all by myself. Remember, I was seven years old. But nothing would stop me. I had witnessed the magic of gliding in moving walls of emerald waters. So I started to work for my dream, and that meant I had to make some sacrifices, and sometimes I wasn't able to hang around with my friends on the old, wise tree. But once in a while, with my pocket money I would buy a surfing magazine. And after each day of work, I would gently cut a page of these magazines and glue it to one of the walls of the room where I slept. I use to call it my "Wall of Dreams" Well-known surfers riding wonderful waves in different corners of the world would stare at me every time I would go to sleep, tired, but happy after working in the hardware store owned by a friend of my grandfather, keeping in order the shop, cleaning the windows, mopping the floor.

Summer went by, and after three months of hard work, I thought I had earned enough money to be able to tell my father I was ready for the "secret pact" we had made. I remember my father's smile, when I gave him most of the money I had earned: the smile of a father proud of his son. "Done deal!" he said. "Next week we'll go and buy the surfboard you want and have worked so hard for."

A week went by, a week that seemed an eternity, and together in his blue Peugeot we headed to the only surf shop that existed at that time in the city where I was born.

Yet, I never imagined that, 25 years later, I would have circled the planet three times, and surfed all the surf spots that I had only been able to imagine in my "Wall of Dreams," and many more…

Dear Daniel,

I have always being an optimist.

In the solitude of my beloved sea, I have found answers to the questions that have always intrigued my soul, Daniel. I have learned to live happily with myself. Sometimes the light of a candle is the only company I need.

Trying to keep my life simple, I have managed to learn the true meaning of life, at least from my point of view. I have been able to enjoy life in all its power after crossing the crystal walls built by society and also by myself: the naked reality, pure, and unique. And more than liking what you see, you learn to love it.

But yet, every time you open a door, you see not only the things you believe in, but also risk the pain and suffering that keeps this wonderful world from being a perfect place for all of us to live in. Some are lucky, some are not. I can't say why, because I don't have the answer. I guess that's part of our human nature: we will always be condemned to make mistakes Patience and humbleness are the strengths that a man needs to recognize his mistakes, failures, as well as his achievements, Daniel.

Yet, despite the suffering I have experienced in my life, I was able to live the life I wanted to live as far and wide as my special relationship with the ocean. Being surfing, diving, just walking bare-foot on the wet sand of the seashore, it always gave me the courage to go on. The ocean taught me to see the bright part of life, Daniel, and stick to it, without avoiding to confront the real tough times I sometimes had to live.

And that's why I am still a believer. I always try to get the best out of the worst. Don't believe those that tell you that things cannot be done; they can. Reality is a state of mind. The path of life is tougher for some, dear Daniel; but in the end some have to suffer more than others to achieve their dreams, their purpose in life. Maybe God has a different mission for all of us. Again, I don't have an answer for why things work this way. I can only tell you that you can try to achieve your goals, no matter how tough the road may seem; because like any human being I have also had my chain of misfortunes, and you probably will, too.

But I have learned a very important lesson, Daniel: the only fight I will lose is the one I am not willing to fight: fear of the unknown is what paralyses the will of a human being. I have never known a human being that doesn't have a problem, be it financial, an illness, family relations, couple relation, or spiritual death. But once you accept your human condition, problems can turn into challenges and opportunities to learn.

Life is like a block of ice that is continually melting away, Daniel. Before it melts completely, try to realize the truth within you.

My only desire while I write these words is your happiness, Daniel. Your happiness is my happiness. Right now, I have no happiness apart from you. But I will always tell you how I've lived, the mistakes I have made, the dreams I have achieved, and the lessons I have learned. Use it only as a guide coming from someone that loves you completely.

But this I can promise you: I will never stand in your way if you decide to live your life in a different way from mine: never. And I will always love you the same, no matter what.

Sergio

V

Winters and summers came and went.

I grew up, surrounded with my great friends from High School. We went surfing almost every day of the year. In winter, we would always try to catch the last rays of Sun during the week, and after finishing school we would rush to the empty cold beaches that lay beneath the cliffs of Lima. Sometimes I would go out by myself, with my wet-suit on, walking barefoot the two blocks that would take me to the dusty trail down the cliff to a surfing beach called Punta Roquitas (Little Rocks Point).

Without hesitating, I would rush into the water, as there was probably one hour of light before dusk settled. Even today, this is the best time for me to go surfing. A time when, arriving by car, I can watch everyone leaving just as the wind starts to blow and the hot sand starts to cool off.

I don't know if these kinds of things marked my life, or maybe I was born that way: always against the flow, arriving when everyone is leaving, preferring to be alone rather than surrounded by the crowds. It has always been the same, even when traveling to faraway lands in search of the perfect wave. Sure, it was wonderful during the summer to surf with my friends in the warm water, staying all day at the beach, sometimes with our girlfriends, and finishing the day with the romantic sunset cuddling and embracing each other, kissing like only youngsters know how to do. Mellow waves, great friends, falling in love and doing all the things that turn that time of your life called youth into a song of joy, a tribute to be alive.

But even though I loved to be with my friends and talk about the waves, smoking our first cigarettes and lighting a fire at the beach at the end of the day (I didn't smoke until the day I went to the movies to see The Exorcist, a mistake I would regret for the rest of my life!); I still preferred the lonely winter days, surfing in the vastness of the ocean, all by myself, sometimes surrounded by dolphins that would keep me company.

Yes; don't ask me why, but I guess I was destined to be a loner, and although I would sometimes feel sad for not having someone to share all those magical moments that I spent, gliding in walls of salty water, I never regret taking that path in my life. In a sense I learnt to live with myself, and I never imagined how many doors that attitude towards life would open as I grew up.

High school came to an end when we graduated one Sunday afternoon; I still remember it as if it were yesterday. I was 16.

The Headmaster of the British School where I studied and spent some of the most wonderful years of my life gave the usual speech, not without mentioning that he had never known any calls as well as he knew us, since all of us at least been in his office at least once for misbehaving! Indeed, we were no angels, and now, looking back, I regret many of the nasty things I did. But we were teenagers, and although we did some bad things, as all teenagers do, we never really meant no harm to anyone.

By that time, my parents had already split. I thought it would be a very traumatic experience at the beginning, but it wasn't, at least for me. I always felt that I preferred to see them happy and at peace living their own separate lives, rather than fighting all the time. Of course, at that time, my brother and I blamed my father for leaving us. But as the years went by, and I grew up and had my own love experiences, I learnt that a relationship between a couple is just that: it is a relationship between two people; that there is no way, no matter how much you know, to say who is guilty and who is not. All human beings are condemned to make mistakes, as it is a part of our essence, but when a relationship between a man and a woman goes wrong, the only two who really know the truth are themselves. We can witness the situations we're caught in, but we will never be able to be completely sure who was wrong and who was right. I guess in the end it is a bit of both, and when they got to a situation that could not be handled anymore, I much preferred to suffer for a while until the storm had passed, instead of watching two persons I loved so much living in a daily agony for the rest of their lives. Yet, I never heard my father talking bad things about my mother, and vice-versa. They were good, decent people.

One year before finishing high school, I had been secretly planning what would come next. Staring at my "Wall of Dreams," with all those pictures of surfers gliding in distant and exotic places, I knew I had to go to surf those faraway waves, but how? Needless to say; I knew I could count with my father to finance my college education overseas. But that was not the point. I wanted to do it by myself. Work hard, earn the money to apply to a university in the U.S.A., and spend all my vacations traveling to places like Hawaii, Mexico, Central America and California. To surf the epic and dangerous waves of the Hawaiian Islands, or go south to Mexico, where people were starting to talk about newly discovered surfing breaks in the middle of the jungle, and why not, tasting the soul surfer spirit of California.

But how would I earn the money to pay all the costs incurred in making such a life come true? I was all by myself. Yet my parents had always taught me that in order to achieve your goals in a decent and practical way, there is only one method: work hard, and with honesty.

Where there's a will, there's always a way; and being a loner, surfing by myself in those windy winter afternoons, going against the flow, without noticing it, I had started to do something without even realizing it at that time. I had started to leave the safety zone: to look outside the box where society wants us to live our lives.

It took a long time for me realize how important these experiences of "breaking the rules" had been. Following my instincts without taking into account what others would tell me was best for me would eventually start turning me into the human being that many years ago started to live his own life, the one he came into this world to live.

Dear Daniel,

I believe that sooner or later life brings us hard time: Daniel: times to test our courage, times to test our faith. It has happened to me, as it happens to every human being. This I learned after growing up and starting to experience the misfortunes that life sometimes challenges us with, because suffering is part of life. Life comes to us as a package, and although we try our best to be as happy as we can, sometimes we must deal with sadness, even defeat; at least for some time.

You are still too young to understand why the love relationship I had with your beautiful mother ended. We have realized we are so different, Daniel. Yet one thing I would ask you: don't judge us. We are just simple human beings that fell in love, and life gave us the most precious treasure of all: You. Yesterday you and I spent a wonderful day in my apartment: we played together for hours, and then we slept side by side, went to the park with Oskar and had a lot of fun. That night, I took you back to your mother's home, and your eyes shone like gold when you saw her. That same night, when you went to bed, totally exhausted after yet another magical day, your mother and I went to have dinner in a very cozy restaurant. We spoke about our day, some problems she had at work, or with her family, and she also listened to my problems, like good friends do.

Your mother and I will be bonded forever Daniel, because sooner rather than later the bad moments fade away, while the wonderful memories last for a lifetime.

But most of all, we have you: the proof of our true love and the biggest treasure life could have given us. But when things don't work as you thought they would, Daniel, I believe it is better to face the storm until the sun appears again, rather than living a life in daily agony.

Your mother and I are not lovers anymore, but we are becoming the best of friends. We don't argue anymore, and that has opened a space to a wonderful friendship. As I said before, the words resentment, hate or enemies are not part of our vocabulary any more.

So we will try our best as human beings for you to understand that, although we don't live together anymore, we have build a "family" in our own and unique special way.

I will always love your mother, Daniel, in a very special way, and I know she will love me too. But you are the most important thing for both of us, and you will always be surrounded by love: always.

Please forgive me for not have been able to provide you with a "normal home" Daniel.

I hope you will.

With true love,

Sergio

VI

Finally the decision was taken: I would study in a university in the United States. How? No idea. I just knew I would.

It is incredible how the pieces of a puzzle start to come together when you take a first step in the right direction in your life. All my friends, after finishing high school, had attended university. Not me. I started to get small jobs, and applied what a very wise person had once said to me: "If you earn one hundred, live with eighty, and look like you only earn fifty." This was: a simple and beautiful rule, at least for me. Once you break the fixation with fine clothes, fancy cars or even the best surfboard, life becomes much simpler, much easier. I've always said this: my most treasured material possessions are still the ones I have learned to live without. When I look around me, and see so many people anxious to buy the last state-of-the-art iPod, the latest Blackberry, the state of art LED flat screen, I come to realize that those things can give you pleasure, but at the same time enslave you. Watching them I also learned another great lesson: the only person you should compete in life with is yourself. So the day I stopped looking at all these fancy things and really focused on my goal, my dream, my life, everything became easier. Simple decisions as: "Should I buy that ice-cream or put the money in my little plastic safe-box?" The answer would almost always be the same: "Remember what you went out to achieve." So little by little, my safe-box got heavier and heavier.

The other thing I did at the same time was browse through the schools that granted scholarships if you kept good grades. In the end, I reduced my list to two choices: Texas A&M University, and the University of San Diego, in California. Needless to say, my dream was to study in California, but it was twice as expensive as the School in Texas. I had to face my economic reality. "Don't forget what you went out to achieve in the first place," I thought to myself. You have worked your butt off for more than a year, and now you have to make a decision. So I decided to attend Texas A&M, one hour away from the closest shore. At the time I didn't understand why I made that decision. But as the years went by, I did understand.

Far from the ocean I loved so much, spending every day of my school break traveling to all those wonderful surf spots I had heard about, made me come to a realization. Living far away from shoreline for the first time in my life made me understand that my love for the ocean was much stronger that I'd ever thought. I promised myself never to forget the sacrifice of being away of the two things I love the most: my mother and the ocean, just to understand how much I really loved them.

And since that time of my existence, I have learnt to enjoy every single breath of life. To understand that life doesn't owe me anything. But if you are willing to conquer the world by following your dreams, big sacrifices will come in the way. But that will give much more value to what you are trying to achieve.

Dear Daniel,

I am going through my old photograph albums, and realize how lucky I have been to live the life I am still living. Because I have gone through really painful moments, moments of immense joy, times of dark storms, and of wonderful sunny skies. Yes Daniel: today, and now, I can say that I have always been alive...

Since I was a kid, Daniel, I believed that dreams could come true. Now, after the years have turned me into a grown-up child, I know that the most important reason we are in this wonderful place called Earth, is to choose the single and unique path that each of us has to travel to make his life worth living. Listening and the dictates of that voice we all have within ourselves: a voice that whispers to our soul who we are, what we want, and which road in life we should take.

But I believe, as I did when I was a child Daniel, that the secret of a happy and fulfilling existence depends on the road you choose, and that that road should be your own road, the one that comes from within your heart.

Only those who dare to go a little further discover how far they can really go. Only those who follow their own path can live a life based in authenticity, love, and harmony. Only those who walk at the sound of their own music are truly free.

Do not follow paths already traveled, my beloved boy: go instead where there is no road, and leave your trail. Make mistakes. Stand up again. Challenge adversity. Find the courage to go on. Make something spectacular of your life!

You only live once Daniel; but if you follow your own road you will discover, when you reach the end of the journey, you will feel you have experienced a thousand lives! Life is beautiful Daniel, no matter what others might tell you. Beauty is in the eye of the beholder, always. So follow your own road, the one nobody has ever traveled before, and leave your trail for the universe and you to rejoice.

Never let your fears stand in the way of your dreams, Daniel. Never!

With much love,

Sergio

VII

I will never forget the day I left my wonderful childhood and my own high school wonder years to travel to the States in search of a dream.

Financially weak but determined to attain my dream, me and my friends gathered in my home before going to airport together: I had mixed feelings: the feeling of fear of the unknown that always precedes a big change in your life; leaving behind my loved ones, especially my mother.

I knew how sad my mother was, but at the same time how proud she was of what I had achieved. "My mission on Earth," she once said to me, "was to pick enough feathers on the sand of the beaches we loved to walk together, knit them as tight as I could, and one day give them to you so you can fly towards your dreams with your own wings" I still keep with me the small book she gave me, dedicated with those words. "Mom, remember it's just a farewell, until we see each other again," I said to her. "I know," she replied, tears in her eyes. "I have prepared all my life for this moment," she said, "so go on wherever you want to go. I will always be here, if you need me."

And at that instant I felt that the "umbilical cord" had broken forever. One human being who had given life and love to another one, for more than 20 years, was now letting go what she used to call "the reason of her life."

Finally it was time to take the plane that would take me to faraway lands. I had been crying with all my friends. The airport was packed, for at that time I was a very sociable person, and had hundreds of friends. After saying good-bye to all of them and kissing my ex-girlfriend, Silvia, the summer love of my life, I stared one more time at all the magical world I was leaving behind, and as if my legs refuse to walk towards the plane terminal, I sent a kiss to all and didn't look back again. The pain was too strong; and that day I learnt, and it has happened through all my life, that always, when you leave a place or someone you love, you die a little.

You know something, Daniel?

While we grow up, and don't ask me when or why, at one point we convince ourselves that life will be better once we start leaving things for the future. We convince ourselves that life will be better once we finish our career, after we get a job, after we get married, after having a child, or maybe two.

But then we feel frustrated because our children have not grown enough, and they are stealing part of our lives: we start to think that we will be happier once they grow up. But then we start complaining that things get more complicated as our children grow up, they start to think with their own minds and sometimes make our life miserable. They rebel against us, and it gets tougher to talk or deal with them. But we say to ourselves: we will be happier when they leave that stage.

Then we start believing that we will be happier once one of the married partners starts to earn more money. When we have the means to purchase a better car, when we can go on holidays, when we reach that better job in our company, when we finally lose those extra kilograms in our belly, or even when we finally retire.

The truth, Daniel, the way I see it, and say this in a very humble way, is that there is no better time to be happier than here and now.

49

If not now, then when? Life will always be full of challenges, of "Ok, let´s leave it for the future." I believe that it is better to admit and decide that the moment to be happy is here and now. There's not a tomorrow, not even a road for happiness. Happiness and the road towards happiness is what we start to build from this moment. Cherish the present. And never forget that time doesn't wait for anyone.

So as you grow up Daniel, never stop waiting until you finish your career, until you fall in love, until you find a good job, until you get married, if that's what you want, or even until you have children. Because one day they will leave the nest, maybe one day you will get divorced. Don't get used to wait for a Friday night, or until Sunday morning, not even for spring, summer winter or fall. Most of all Daniel, don't wait until you die to realize that there is no better moment to be happy than right now! Happiness is on the own trail you walk, as well as in reaching the dreams you went out to achieve.

As I read somewhere, long time ago;

Work as if you didn't need the money

Love as if you had never gotten hurt,

And dance as if nobody's watching

That is life!

Your father,

Sergio

VIII

Studying in a foreign country taught me many wonderful life lessons.

Texas A&M has a large international community of students. Although it was founded initially as a military school, female students were accepted several years after its foundation. As the international community grew, it turned into a truly cosmopolitan school.

I made friends from all the corners of the world, from Asia, the Middle East, from Israel, from Africa, from Europe and Canada, and of course from Latin America and the U.S. If you have an open mind, you can make friends anywhere!

At the beginning I slept at the dormitories on campus. It was cheaper. I had Spanish roommates, U.S. roommates, Muslim roommates: the lot. And I realized that in the end we are all simple human beings, born in different lands with different traditions and religions. And I realized that those were the reasons that made us think differently: traditions, different faiths. For the rest, we are all the same: unique human creatures that could live in much more harmony if we realized that no matter where you were born, or what the color of your skin is, or what religion you practice, if any, our blood is always red.

I wanted to live outside the campus. So I started working first in the university's restaurant. Then, I painted apartments and lined soccer fields with white chalk in freezing conditions. But so much hard work finally paid off, and saving some money and at the same time obtaining a scholarship, I was ready to start traveling to all these wonderful beaches that I wanted to surf.

When I finally moved off-campus, I shared a small house with three Brazilian surfers. As I only went back to my country once a year for Christmas, we would take advantage of the rest of the holidays to go surfing. First on the list was California, where we drove up the famous US 1, a highway that meanders through the entire Californian coast. We surfed from San Diego all the way to Santa Cruz and even further. Then we went twice to Hawaii, home of the most powerful and dangerous waves in the world. I almost drowned more than once, and often cut myself on coral and reefs. But nothing ever stopped me from gliding in new and exotic walls of pure salty water, sometimes with dolphins as companions, or maybe the odd whale, even sharks!

During the last two years of study in the States we traveled to Mexico, to the giant waves of Puerto Escondido, or the longest waves in the world in San Blas, taking a train, driving, hitch-hiking, staying in houses of girls that we met, even camping in the middle of the jungle, surrounded by the biggest iguanas I have ever seen, making sure that the tent was tightly closed, in case a poisonous spider or snake was lurking around! Life was an adventure, full of danger and not knowing what tomorrow would bring. But no matter what, we felt alive.

After four years of studying, working hard and surfing some of the most awesome waves in the world, I became a chemical engineer. At that time I was in love with a lovely girl from Colombia, and having finished school meant we would have to split. The day I said farewell to her, to all the wonderful friends I had made, and to a place that had embraced me so close the last four years, my mind became filled with memories. I realized that every time you have to say goodbye, and go on with your life, in a sense you die a little. A part of you remains in the place forever: the same way I felt when I left the city I was born to follow a dream in the States. Now, returning to the country where I was born and to my family, I felt the same lump in my throat.

And I learned that my life would be filled with lots of small dying moments, if I wanted to live the live I had decide to live: that spreading memories through the winds of faraway lands would help me make my personal journey a better place to be.

HOLA PAPÁ
Te quiero mucho.
no se. que me lleves al
Regatas.
Que lindo papá.
Tu casa que linda es.
Espero que dani este bien
Te quiero ♥

DANIEL

Letter from Daniel.

Dear Daniel,

The peace that I carry in my heart is totally different to the peace I dreamt of when I was young.

When I was young, I thought being in peace was doing whatever I wanted, keeping quiet, and always trying to avoid facing my own contradictions or a sad situation.

Now, looking back throughout the years my beloved Daniel, I can say that at least for me, the peace that I carry in my heart is the result of some important lessons that life has given me. Peace for me means to be in harmony with the universe that surrounds me, accepting the good and bad things that life places in front of me. It means accepting challenges, good and the bad times, and always having faith that sooner or later the storm will pass and the sun will shine again. Peace means being in harmony with your inner self, accepting who you are, and realizing that as a human being you will be condemned to make mistakes. Peace is a synonym for humility. Assuming responsibilities and doing the job, feeling serene in the face of adversity.

Living in peace is respecting other ways of thinking, giving much, much more than what you get. It is the will to share what I possess, to accept the things I cannot change, courage to change the things I can, and having the wisdom to know the difference, admitting that sometimes I am wrong. It's knowing and understanding that some day, I will harvest what I cultivated throughout my life.

Set your heart free of any envy or hate, Daniel, and never be worried about what the future might bring: live in simplicity and serendipity, give a lot and expect very little. Travel a lot and see the world with your own eyes, and wonder at what you see. Never get used to be alive, Daniel.

...and never lose faith or your energy to strive for a better spiritual life Daniel.

I love you, Daniel!

Your father.

IX

So what next?

I finally got back to the city I was born in and to those wonderful cliffs that had been so important to me in the first years of my life; and I sat once again, my legs clinging free towards the rough oceans that loomed fifty meters below me. I surfed as if there was no tomorrow.

Sometimes my mother would come with me, and we would stay hours, talking about life, just staring at beautiful sunsets or multicolored sunrises. It felt good to be close to her, physically speaking, because during my stay in the States I had never stopped thinking about her. We would remember the times when she went to visit me to Texas, and how happy she would feel about seeing her small child turn into what she called a "grown-up child."

But she knew me too well. She knew I wouldn't stay for long. Being the soul surfer and nomad that I was, traveling to some wonderful developed places, and also to some exotic ones, had only increased my appetite to keep moving, to discover new worlds, new surfing beaches, to see things with my own eyes instead of watching them on TV or via the photographs that someone else had shown me. I wanted to discover the world through my own experiences. And who could know me better than the wonderful human being that had taken care of me in her tender womb, taught me to appreciate the simple things of life, the really important ones, and who had known from the beginning that your children come to the world through you, but their dreams live in the future, and that she could only love me, guide me, teach me, but never own me?

It's amazing when you realize that some small seemingly unimportant things that happen in your life can change your destiny forever.

I had already settled in the city, and my first job was selling industrial products for a multinational company. My boss was one of the gentlest persons I had ever met, and working with him seemed a breeze. I was happy with my job, but that didn't mean that I would stay there forever. My plans to live my life had probably been decided long before I was born: I just had to have the courage to follow the voice of my heart; and I knew that something would soon occur. In the meantime, being with my high school friends, spending some time with my mother, falling in love, surfing with dolphins, I had no regrets while I stayed at "home." I wasn't in a hurry.

It happened one afternoon as I was cleaning my "memory lane" drawer, a place where I had kept little things that one way or another had touched my life forever. Letters from Silvia, my one and only summer love, my first savings account statements, little toys that I had cherished so much when I was a baby, photographs of my first surfing rides. Some books, just a few, that had touched my life since I read them, like The Little Prince or The Prophet.

I was immersed in my memories when I felt something metallic fell to the floor. At first I didn't recognize it. Only when I picked it up did I realize what it was: the golden kangaroo pin that my teacher in kindergarten had given me as a present on my first day of class. I couldn't believe I still had it! So I got a clean piece of cloth, sat on my bed and polished it. But what I didn't realize was that, the more I touched it and saw it, some internal chemistry began working inside my brain.

It sparkled like gold. It was so small, yet so precious. A little golden kangaroo, symbol of a faraway land called Australia.

You have to go. And I did...

But not long after, tragedy struck.

My mother Olga at her first communion.

Dear Daniel,

I think what I'm about to tell you is among the best pieces of advice I will ever be able to give you. Take it if you choose to.

In the society in which we were born, when a loved one dies, it's a real tragedy, something so different to other cultures I have seen, where dying is just seen as the beginning of a new life, a re-birth in a better world. In these cultures, people celebrate when a loved one passes away. Don't get me wrong. I am not saying it is not tragic when a son or daughter dies before their parents. It's traumatic because in some way the rules of the universe have been twisted. I have seen friends who have lost their siblings, and from what I have heard there is no stronger pain in the world. It shouldn't happen. But unfortunately sometimes it does. Why? Questions for the wind, Daniel; I don't have all the answers.

Yet what I am referring to are the people around us that love us and that we love Daniel, and with whom we share most of our time; friends parents, grandparents. It is normal in the society where we live for families to fight. But one thing that saddens me is that most people take their loved ones for granted.

Not me, Daniel. I was lucky to understand that "I love you," "thanks for being who you are," should be said every day of our lives, to the ones you love. So instead of waiting for someone to die and for everyone to start crying, and of course arrange a "decent" burial, all dressed in black, whether the person who died is not in that body anymore, spread love, kisses and kind words every single day of your life.

To my father, who is in good health but lives in another country, I dedicated a book, "Tales from the Heavens" a way to say thanks for opening my eyes to a wonderful world, thanks to his intelligence, patience and curiosity, and the lessons he taught me. I also called him to thank him for having being such an important part of my life.

But I guess the most important thing I have done in my life is, before leaving for Australia, I called my mother to tell her I was going to visit her. We drove in her car and we parked in front of the ocean, a place we both loved. "What is the special occasion?" she asked me.

"No special occasion," I answered to her. "I just wanted to be close to you, look at your beautiful emerald eyes, and just kiss you and say:

Thank you for being my mother. Life blessed me with the best mother in the world.

Tears started to run down down her cheeks. When she regained her composure, after hugging me for a long time, without saying a single word, she held my face with her two tender hands, and, looking me into the eyes, she said;

"What you have just said and done, my beloved Sergio is the best present I have ever received in my life. Because for a mother to hear her son say the words you just said, it means everything we went through in this journey called life was worth it, my son. That I did my job, with so much love that you will never understand until one day when you have children of your own. What you just said, Sergio has made me feel that my life had a reason stronger than all other reasons. No matter what the future may bring, this moment we are sharing

right now, for me, as a mother, will be the most important day of my life. The day someone who I consider the reason for my life said to me: "Thanks for being my mother."

Seize the day, Daniel: Spread hugs, kisses and love to everyone around the world every day. Don't assume others know what you feel for them. Say it. It makes a huge difference. Giving something, without asking anything in return; the best present you can get throughout your life, Daniel.

And one month before I left for Australia, Daniel, your grandmother died of a stroke.

I wish you could have met her. You two would have been inseparable!

Sergio

Happy times in Australia.

X

My years in Australia were among the most beautiful periods of my life. And I learned a lesson I have never forgotten: happiness is not always at the end of the journey, but sometimes in the journey itself. Traveling to Australia from South America takes you almost a day just flying! So I decided that as the plane made several stops along the way, I would rest in those places, not only to make the trip more comfortable, but also to discover new lands. I stopped at Easter Island, and discovered the beautiful statues of Rapa Nui. The island's surf was incredible, though once in a while a white shark would linger nearby.

My next stop was Tahiti, the famous tropical islands in the middle of the South Pacific. Suddenly I was immersed in the French culture and the world of crepes. I don't think I have ever been to a hotter place, with temperatures hovering around forty degrees Celsius both day and night. With its crystalline coral reefs and huge tropical mountains, its people who live at a much slower pace, and its crown jewel, Bora-Bora, Tahiti is a fairy tale island. Swimming with the dolphins in the inner lagoon, I couldn't have felt happier. More than that, seeing magnificent sunsets that I had never seen before and surfing beaches where the sand was pitch black due to its volcanic origin, I realized that by watching nature and the rhythms at which it moved, I was discovering the true essence of our Mother Earth. But more important than anything else, I was discovering the world with my own eyes, not someone else's.

And without even noticing, I was also making an internal journey, one that would show me who I was, what I wanted, and the true purpose of my life.

After spending a week in Tahiti, it was time to catch the plane that would take me to Auckland, New Zealand. Again, just by stepping off the plane, I was immersed in a totally different culture, built basically by British immigrants and the local Maoris, two wonderful cultures that had melted together to build the most peaceful country on Earth.

I stayed in New Zealand several days, and surf the icy waters of the Northern Island. New Zealand is one of the only places in the world where you can surf in beautiful clear waters, and see snow-capped mountains at the same time. If Australia is known as "the lucky country," New Zealand is known as the best place in the world to raise a family. Crime is virtually non-existent, and life flows peacefully with the change of seasons. Definitely a Paradise for children and grown-up children! I traveled to the South Island, and swam with thousands of dolphins in a small town called Kaikoura. I went camping into the rainforests, staying for days, meditating and learning from Nature

Needless to say, I did all this alone, just with the company of my best friend: myself. And I learnt that if you are able to be at peace with yourself and not feel lonely, you have truly made a great leap into living a life of peace and tranquility: if you trust your instincts, and life as it is, and if you are lucky enough, one day you will be able to live peacefully not only when you are surrounded by the things you love, but also when the going gets tough. It's all in your mind!

After staying a few days in the "land of the long cloud," as New Zealand is known, I was ready to catch the last plane that would take me to my final destination: Australia.

After putting all my stuff together, I gazed for the last time at the snow-capped mountains of New Zealand, its temperate rain forests, its wonderful people.

I felt alive…

Dear Daniel,

I have learned in life that you don't have the right to judge anyone: just yourself.

While you grow up Daniel, you will realize that we are all victims of victims. That sometimes your parents want you to achieve what they never achieved. Or maybe they were born in a family with strict rules, and human behavior will tell their children to live the way they lived: it's not their fault Daniel; at least not all of it.

Many human beings have had traumatic situations in their lives: wars, child abuse, being bullied when they were small, and these have marked their lives. Unfortunately, sometimes these experiences are passed onto their own children and that's where all the mess starts.

When you were born, your mother and I made a promise to let you be whatever you wanted to be. Nobody is born a father, or a mother. It's something you learn along the way. So forgive us for the mistakes we will make with you. We are just human beings, maybe older than you, but in the end, the same.

The other day I received from a good friend this beautiful poem I want to share with you. It really made me understand that we all have a life to live, and we all have the duty to let others live their own lives, the one they have chosen. Nobody owns the whole truth. Not one single human being. So again, forgive me for the mistakes I will make, because I will make them. I hope they aren't many!

I hope in some way that it will help you understand the way I see and feel life, and the way I have lived my life, and keep living it. When I read it, it was as if I was talking about myself, and it comforted me, because although I don't know who wrote it, it feels good knowing that there is someone out there that thinks and feels the same way, and that somehow, is traveling through his life the same way I am traveling through mine.

It goes like this:

"Being old is that who has lived many years,

But feeling old is that who has lost the joy of feeling alive.

Being old turns you a bit slower,

But feeling old kills the dreams of you spirit...

Being old is asking yourself: "is it really worth it?"

Feeling old is answering "no" without even thinking about it.

Being old is when you dream when you're awake.

Feeling old is when you can barely sleep at night.

Being old means there are still many things to learn and discover.

Feeling old is not learning or teaching anything.

Being old is exercising your body, lifting your spirit, having dreams.

Feeling old is watching the TV sitting in, a couch all day... and the next day... and the next.

Being old means having a future you have planned

Feeling old means your agenda is blank, and you only remember "the good old days."

Being old means trying something new every day, renewing yourself, placing your eyes in the horizon, trying to find out what lies far ahead.

Feeling old is starting to think that maybe today is the last day of your life, and closing yourself once again in the "safety zone."

So being old is not an age; Daniel: it's in the way you approach life. But feeling old: well you can still be a teenager and already feel old, if you don't live one day at a time, if you stop dreaming, if you sell your spirit to the comfort of what's safe.

Think about it Daniel, a small advice from a grown-up child to another one that is still taking his first steps in the journey of life: to grow up, or to become old-it's your decision Daniel.

I wish someone had shared this with me when I was just starting to live, Daniel. That's why I feel so happy that I can share it with you, even though you still cannot read. But you will learn, one day.

I hope it helps you!

Your father.

XI

Australia is among the few countries that look more beautiful when you're there. Pictures and post-cards don't do it justice. The colors are so intense. A country the size of the United States, populated by fewer than twenty million people and millions of parrots, kangaroos of all kinds, raccoons, possums and eucalyptus forest, rain forests that go on forever: it's true paradise for nature lovers and those seeking a peaceful lifestyle. It is a breeze of freshness for all our senses, with the feeling so palpable you can almost breathe it: no matter what, everything will be okay in the end. A country where fair play rules, and populated mainly by Irish, Scottish and English descendants, but with an array of communities that came from all over the world to follow a dream.

But what really dazzled me about Australia was its ocean, from the deep blue colors of the Tasmanian Sea to the emerald crystal waters of its multi-colored coral reefs. You could camp on an isolated island or beach for days, just with the company of the stars, the possums and the kangaroos. "The Lucky Country," from my point of view, is an understatement of this piece of Paradise that God placed in the world and whose people have learned to preserve probably as the most unspoiled country on Earth.

Needless to say, at that time, I never knew I was about to make one of the biggest – if not the biggest – mistakes of my life:

a mistake that would throw me into the shadows of a life without meaning, without purpose; a mistake that almost cost me my life, in the sense of almost forgetting who I was and disappearing once and for all inside the box.

I got a great job as an executive sales manager in a company that built steel plants throughout the region. Working mainly from home, I arranged my day depending on sea swells generated by the Roaring Forties, which stem directly from low-pressure systems that form in the Southern Ocean and gently bent towards the eastern coast of Oz. Since I was free to set my own schedule, if a swell arrived say, a Tuesday morning, I could safely go surfing and return home in time to do the work of the company that had hired me. More than that, I could work during the weekends when there were no waves, and have the time to surf every time a swell hit the coast. It was an ideal job for someone like me that never got used to working from 8 a.m. to 5 p.m. So long as I did my work, I could come and go as I pleased during the day. During my holidays, I would head straight to Indonesia, Fiji, New Caledonia or the Mentawai Islands, where I surfed some of the most wonderful waves of my life.

One afternoon, the president of the company called me from the U.K. He wanted me to go and see him. When I arrived to the U.K. we spoke for more than an hour. Basically, they were very happy with my performance and were now offering to put me in charge of the whole region, which included Australia, New Zealand and Southeast Asia. The offer came with a huge salary increase – I almost fell from the chair when they told me. On top of that, I would be able to travel through many exotic countries, and the new job, of course, came with all the "perks" that would make the offer almost impossible to reject: flying first class, staying in five star hotels, a luxury house in the best area of Sydney, a very expensive car for my personal use, and all kind of luxuries that came with a CEO job. I was thirty-three years old, and people would congratulate me or feel envy for having climbed so fast on the "ladder of success" in my short career. But deep within myself, I was more excited imagining I would be able to surf places like Vietnam, the Philippines, Japan, and finally achieve my dream of having surfed through all the best surfing spots of the world!

Sadly, sooner than later I'd realize that accepting the job was probably the worst mistake of my life. Though I couldn't have imagined it, I had placed myself in a golden cage and almost lost the most precious gift I believe every human being should have: time to live.

Dear Daniel,

The most terrible darkness is not the one that clouds our eyes and makes us blind, but the one we harbor in the deepest recesses of our heart. Likewise, the brightest light is not the one that bathes the outside of our bodies, but the one that burns from the open pits of the heart and glows warmly through the eyes. Let this light guide you to the fulfillment of your destiny.

I have learned that here on earth some people might be able to stand out because of their abilities. But I have also realized that the happiest human beings are not those who have been able to stand out, but those that have followed the voice of their heart. Love yourself for what you are. Never compare yourself to others; that is not the reason you are on Earth. Deal with your advantages and disadvantages, and make of your life a song of joy. But never forget Daniel that to be fully happy, you must sometimes be brave. Make life not only a song, but also a melodious prayer that enriches your spirit. Try to discover that light that comes from your interior. Don't count your misfortunes — count your blessings. Sooner or later, you will make mistakes, like I did, and probably will keep making them. More than that: we have the duty to help those who are living through their own private hell. We have to let them know what we have already learned, Daniel: hold on tight while you suffer, because sooner or later your suffering will end, if you are willing to take tough decisions. How can you shine if you don't clash with the darkness? It is with much effort and work that we strengthen our souls, and one day you will realize that your sadness is made of thin air. Nobody should be sad for the mistakes he or she has already made. Forgiveness of one's self is essential in order to be at peace with the world.

Never forget it Daniel: you are the sole maker of your destiny.

With much light,

Sergio

XII

At the start, I was truly happy with my new position and ready to keep moving up in my career.

One of the first things I noticed was that most of the salary increase I got was part of a package. The company would pay me the rent of a beautiful house on the cliffs of the Northern Beaches of Sydney. I also had a private parking space below one of the tall skyscrapers of Sydney Business and Financial Center. I wasn't driving a Ford Falcon anymore, I now had a Lexus; much more expensive, all courtesy of the Company. To put the icing on the cake, they gave me as a gift a golden Rolex, a very fancy Mont Blanc pen, and a Qantas VIP pass for all its lounges in all the airports of the world. Needless to say, traveling tourist class was out of the question: first class, and if there was no first class, well, I would have to live with Business Class.

My first assignment was to travel to Thailand, where one of the country's tycoons wanted us to build some steel mills for him.

Dressed in my new Armani suit, I waited in the Qantas lounge as I went through the paperwork we had been preparing in Sydney in order to make a presentation in Bangkok.

One of the things I immediately noticed was that many of the people at the lounge were important executives, reading their Financial Times, or maybe the Wall Street Journal. On the walls, big screens with quotations from the most important stock markets of the world kept blinking as stock quotes changed every minute. Everyone wore a fancy tie, was having a drink or working on their laptop, just like me.

But then I noticed what was really bugging me. Nobody talked. Everyone was so concentrated on his own work that they probably didn't notice the presence of the rest of us. They must be very busy, doing very important things, I thought. So I just went back to my numbers. But I was bored, and knew exactly how I was going to present the project. So I grabbed a magazine about Thailand, and started to investigate this exotic country.

I was amazed with what I saw: a place called Chiang Mai, where you could see wild tigers in the rain forests from on top of an elephant! Pukhet, an emerald crystal water Eden where you could dive with manta rays and shark whales all year round. I started to get more and more excited. So I decided that once I finished with the business I had planned in Thailand I'd take a week to visit these fantastic places.

Suddenly a lovely lady came up. "Your plane is about to leave. You can board now." We were the last to board the plane, of course. We were flying first class, and first class flyers don't stand in line. In no time, all the top-of-the-line passengers immediately opened their laptops again. An eight-hour flight! Too much time to waste: to my right, a lady covered in make-up was sipping some Moet Chandon champagne from a crystal glass.

Flying first class, surrounded by beautiful people, I really thought we were superior to those behind the closed curtains in tourist. And for a moment it felt good. Finally all the hard work of the last four years had paid off. I was part of an "elite group," the ones used to having the most expensive material treasures, and the feeling that money can buy it all. Even happiness. Well, maybe they were right, and I had to find out.

So I passed the next three years of my life playing the role of a business- man. Venturing through the most luxurious hotels and restaurants and getting the best material possessions money could buy.

I closed many deals in different countries. This caused a lot of envy with some of my colleagues. But I knew I had an edge, something sometimes they couldn't handle: I wasn't afraid of money or big entrepreneurs.

Let me try to explain myself: if I had to negotiate a deal in, say, Kuala Lumpur, in Malaysia, I would prepare myself mentally by trying to get all the information I could about the entrepreneur I was going to meet. Once I knew the person I was to deal with, I'd prepare my presentation. After finishing, I'd lay back in my chair, and listen. I was never alone; I always had an assistant or two. When the negotiation started, numbers started to come out. Sometimes we would talk about hundreds of millions of dollars, and that's where I could see that some of my colleagues would start to get nervous. They couldn't handle the numbers. It was too much money. On top of that, the tycoon sitting in front of us was an expert in negotiating and trying to lower the price, surrounded by several of his top employees. He was the rich guy; we were only managers working for a big multinational company. Some of these tycoons have a modus operandi I've seen many times: first, they try to convince you who is the boss, the decision-maker; next, they subtly tell you that if you are not willing to accept their offer, they'll take their business somewhere else; finally, surrounded by eight or ten of their top guns, they try to make you feel inferior and under pressure. And I have seen it works with most people. I could see some of my colleagues sweating just by the thought of losing the contract; their legs trembling as they watched the boards in which numbers with many, many zeroes and the U.S. dollar symbol in front were probably too much for them to handle.

My approach was totally different. Sitting in my comfortable chair, I just listened. But deep in my mind I was making a map of this man's life. Probably in his mid fifties or sixties, he would call his beautiful twenty-something secretary to bring some more coffee or tea. Wearing a Rolex covered with diamonds, and wearing a suit that had cost thousands of dollars, with a state of the art Mercedes Benz awaiting him in the parking lot, with a chauffeur and body guards, and sitting at the head of the table in a chair that was slightly higher than all others, surrounded by people he had been able to buy with money, who would never object to any of his comments, even if he was wrong. I tried to imagine his life.

He was definitely cheating on his wife, just by the looks he exchanged with his secretary. His wife probably didn't care, as long as she was a member of the best Country Club in the country, probably had a tennis trainer (who probably didn't just teach tennis!) eating only in the best restaurants, and probably flying in her own private jet.

This was my trick: I would close my eyes for an instant, undress the guy of all the fancy things he had covered himself with, lower his chair in my mind, and pretend just for a moment that the numbers on the dash board were part of a game of Monopoly. It always worked. Once I opened my eyes again, I would now see an old man, with a belly so huge that I couldn't imagine how much fat he had been able to place in his fragile body, a lean body he hadn't exercised for God knows for how many years and someone who had a chip stuck in his head repeating that money could buy everything: a man with no principles or even decency, treating others like garbage, truly believing he owned the truth, and who knows, maybe the world!

I pitied him. What a waste of life! I didn't judge him, don't get me wrong: but this was a man who had to cover himself with all kind of fancy toys so no one could see who he really was. "If he could only take time once in a while to smell the roses," I thought.

An hour later, after he finished talking, I stood up. I knew exactly what I was up against. I thanked him for his brilliant words, asked him for a few minutes to re-calculate our offer and lower the price (of course I was faking; before getting to the meeting I already knew what our last offer would be), and then re-wrote some new numbers on the board, giving him a big discount on our initial offer. Tough entrepreneur he was, he told me it was still too expensive. I smiled. "Well," I said, looking him straight into his eyes, "this is the best offer we can give you. We can guarantee we will build a state of the art steel mill for your company, and that your future business will be very profitable. You will have the best product in the market, at a very reasonable price.

"Still too expensive!" he said. "Make us a better offer!"

Without sitting down again, I started to place all my pens, calculators and paperwork in my work folder. I asked my assistants to do the same, then we shook hands with everyone at the table, and finally I went to where the boss was standing, shook his hand, thanked him for his precious time, and said:

"This is the best we can do. We will be staying in the city

for a week, as we have to visit other customers who are also waiting for a quote from us to build their projects. Thanks again for your time."

I turned around, asked my assistants to follow me. We left the premises.

"How do you do it?" asked Richard, one of my loyal assistants and a one of the best civil engineers I have ever met in my life.

"Do what?" I asked.

"How did you keep your nerve when we were risking losing a contract worth millions of dollars for us?"

"For us, you said? You mean, for the company we work for..."

"Same thing," answered Richard.

"Not at all," I said. I asked the lady at the lobby of the hotel to bring me a second double scotch. I stared at my friend:

"Think, Richard. What is the worst that can happen?"

"We will lose the contract."

"And…?"

"We could lose our jobs!"

"And…?"

He got mad. "Why do you keep saying and? This is no joke!"

I had another sip of my scotch. "Of course is not a joke," I said. "Try to see it this way, Richard: we have already played all our cards, we have given him the best offer we were allowed to give. We have done our job, and on top of that, we had to listen to a miserable alpha male that thinks he owns the world because everything that surrounds him can be purchased with money. So, if he rejects the offer, there's nothing we can do. That we can lose our jobs? Maybe Richard, but you're one of the best engineers I have ever met in my life. If you lose this job, be sure many other companies will be eager to hire you. I'm sure they will! But think positive. Why shouldn't they accept the offer? We don't know what they are discussing, or thinking. So having said all these things, do you think it is worth getting stressed for something we cannot control? Losing this contract won't be the end of the world Richard, and you know it. It's fear of the unknown that makes you sweat!"

"You're right," he said. "It's just that we have so much pressure from the office...

"That's their problem, not yours," I replied.

"Whatever you say," answered Richard, still feeling uncomfortable.

"Come on, relax, have another drink. Anyway, tomorrow we will have an answer."

"Ok," he said.

I called the waitress and asked for another double scotch. I felt even more relaxed.

After drinking my last scotch, we called it a night.

The next morning I woke up with a terrible headache. It was 11 a.m.! How could I have slept so long? I jumped out of bed, and took a couple of aspirins for the painful headache

I was walking towards the bathroom when I saw an envelope under the door. I opened it.

"Please give us a call. Let's make an appointment for this afternoon with our lawyers to close the deal. Your company's offer has been accepted." I smiled. I called Richard to give him the good news before taking a shower.

However, all that coolness I had shown during the meeting the day before, and with my colleagues at the hotel bar would be the result of having accepted the "dream" job. I was feeling lonely, bored; I missed surfing so much and having the time to do the things I loved to do. But I hadn't realize yet that the true reason I felt so relaxed was the fact that every time I would start to feel stressed, I would eliminate my stress by having a drink, or two.

Sadly, my father, being a psychiatrist never told me that genetically we had a propensity for addictions. I don't judge him: it wasn't his fault. But without noticing it, I was about to cross that imaginary line that turns social drinking into a disease called alcoholism, a disease I was born with. It was just a matter of time before it kicked in.

Dear Daniel,

So finally the dark night settled in my life, dear Daniel, I began drinking in excess.

In the beginning, I couldn't accept this terrible reality of life. Bad things happened to others Daniel, not to me. For some reason, at one stage of my life I thought I was invincible. I guess we all think the same. With our whole future in front of us, we believe we are destined to be happy forever. But as experience teaches us, this is certainly not true.

Some time ago, as I've written you, life placed that challenge in front of me, Daniel. The person I loved most in this world suddenly died in my arms. I still remember it as if it had happened yesterday, but it's been more than 13 years. How time flies!

I had read all those stories about people dying in car accidents, in war, even in shootings, or in hospital; I also vaguely remembered my grandfather's funeral, but that was as close to death as I had ever been. With my mother, your grand-mother, it was different. She passed away in my arms, and for the first time in my life I realized that people really died. At least they leave their body. That's what I felt with her. Yet night after night, I begged for her to come back and stay with me, even for just a short time. But she didn't.

I will never forget that horrible feeling of abandonment that haunted my life for the next few years, Daniel. First, I lost my faith in God. How could He take the life of someone so precious, a human being so good, at such a young age, instead of all the bad people that are allowed to grow old? I could no longer believe in a God as unjust as that.

Next, I fell into a deep depression from which I couldn't recover for several years. Worse, my drinking increased dramatically trying to cover my pain.

Huge mistake, Daniel! The values on which I had tried to build a decent life started to crumble. It was like I had fallen into the deepest abysses of hell. The joy of my life was over. Why keep on living?

But now, looking back at that terrible time of my life when I finally accepted complete defeat towards my disease, and asked for help, I can clearly see the one thing that kept me alive: hope. Hope that sooner or later, things would change for the better. Although my life was hell and I couldn't see the light at the end of the tunnel, I knew that I had to fight to survive. As I said before, the only fight you cannot win is the one you are not willing to fight. And the only dream that you cannot make come true is the one you cease to dream.

When I was finally able to look back more objectively on those sad years, I realized that I had made a terrible misjudgment: by blaming God for the death of my mother, I had condemned myself to a life without faith. I had tried to play God by judging God.

How arrogant I was, Daniel! Who did I think I was? God? And yet, after the storm passed, I discovered something very important: I had to learn to be humble. Believe me Daniel: to be humble makes you stronger, not weaker.

It took me some time to accept it, but in the end I succumbed to my disease. So I asked for help, Daniel: and that's when the first rays of sun appeared in the distant horizon. People who shared the same *problem told me that I wasn't responsible for my sickness, but surely I was responsible for my recovery. And I prayed for true humility. I prayed for forgiveness. For I believe it is when you are truly humble, when you grab someone's hand, asking for help, a hand that feels stronger and can hold you, and not let you fall — that is when you start to discover that the best days are yet to come. Despite the death of a loved one, abuse of drugs or alcohol, a job with no purpose, any disease or any other strong and devastating pain, sooner or later you learn that the pain must eventually stop, because it cannot go any deeper. You have touched rock bottom. Then, and only then, do you start to realize that you have a second chance to rebuild your life, if you take it and ask for help. Finally the dark clouds start to dissipate, and the first rays of the new Sun illuminate your future. A rebirth of your soul has begun, anchored by an acceptance of the way things are.*

I remember well one idea that would revolve over and over in my mind when I felt so depressed, so alone, so many years ago.

Why did it happen to me?

Why me?

But when the first glimpse of the new Sun started to warm my cold days, another question popped into my head. Why not me? Am I above the laws of Nature? Am I so arrogant to think that I should be free of suffering, pain and sorrow, while other human beings are not?

And I understood something very important, beautiful Daniel: pain is part of life. Desperation is part of life. Sometimes touching rock bottom is part of life. But it is definitely not the end of life. It is just the beginning of something bigger and spiritually richer than anything I had experienced before.

Just as age is only a trick of time, so is pain just one aspect of life. Happiness and peace of spirit and mind can be achieved; no matter how deeply lost one may feel. Time cures everything Daniel, but you have to be patient. It doesn't happen in an instant or in a day. But the time you least expect it, it happens. And when it happens, something extraordinary occurs: you stop fighting against your fate. You accept your life as it is, and instead of trying to push for what you want, you just let life guide you to your destiny. You start to live with what life gives you, one day at a time.

Total defeat and acceptance of your reality, Daniel: the starting point for a rich spiritual life that will let you take advantage of all the good things that you still have and begin to recover the things that can still be recovered. But to do that, you first have to learn to accept yourself for what you are.

Then, and only then, will you feel that you have been born again. Living one day at a time: enjoying one moment at a time, accepting hardships as the pathway to peace. Accepting this sometimes painful world as it is, not as you would have it be. Trusting that God, or whatever you want to call him, will make all things right if you surrender to his will. In this way, not only will you be happy in this life, but supremely happy forever in the next.

So Daniel, please be very careful: drugs or alcohol abuse can seem as a pleasant alternative to avoid pain or the tough reality of life; but in the end you run the risk of destroying everything you have built. Live with the pain, and face it. Only time will be able to cure your scars, and heal the wounds of your heart.

I lived in hell for a while Daniel. Don't do it. The pain is terrible.

With all my sincerity, my son,

Sergio

XIII

So that was the way my life went for the next few years.

Remembering that gray part of my existence, one without purpose, living a life that was not the life I was meant to live, people around me congratulating me for all the "great things" I had achieved, I recall feeling lonelier than ever, totally lost. I had completely lost the real essence of my existence.

But I knew I had no one to blame. It was my entire fault. I had succumbed to the rat race, and become part of it. Surfing, watching sunsets, even stopping to see a hummingbird were "irrelevant" things that I had stopped doing for what felt like an eternity. Without noticing, I had placed myself in a golden cage, trapped like a bird with clipped wings, doing the same thing day after day, week after week, year after year.

I am a living example of a human being that can touch rock bottom, feel totally lost, and still battle the storm. You feel like you're in a deep pitch-black hole, yet just when you feel there's nothing you can do, a flash of enlightenment pulls you out of the miserable existence you've created for yourself.

It happened while I was closing yet another business deal, this one in a Singapore skyscraper. I guess we all have experiences that for some reason will always stay in the hard drive of our memory, because every time I talk or remember those few minute that changed my life for good, it feels like it had been this morning – although more than a decade has passed. I can still smell the clean air of the hotel; remember the color of the walls of the room I was in. It's like a movie that will stay with me forever.

I was on the 22nd floor in downtown Singapore. I had been in the city for a week, and had mainly traveled to close a deal I had been working on for more than a year. After preparing my final Power Point presentation, we had all of the paperwork on the table, our company lawyers at my side, the customer's lawyers at the other side of the table. We signed the paperwork that had been fully reviewed by our Legal Department, and we would probably end the meeting in half an hour, once we had made sure that everything was in order and settled. This time our client was an Indonesian tycoon.

I remember standing up to walk around the table in order to shake hands with everyone gathered at the meeting. And suddenly it happened. As I was going back to my chair after shaking hands with everyone, I happened to look out the window of the tall glass building. I could see the ocean, all the way to the horizon, and a feeling I hadn't felt in ages rose up from my deepest inner parts:

And I heard a voice, a beautiful voice coming from inside of me, soft, but strong at the same time:

"What are you doing with your life Sergio?"

"Who is that?" I asked.

"It's you: the true you; the child who at seven years of age stood on a surf board for the first time."

I started to sweat. I loosened my tie. I felt I needed air. Later I would realize I was suffering a panic attack.

I had to get out of there. The room seemed to be shrinking, getting smaller, too crowded. It felt like that my colleagues were not talking, they were yelling.

I needed space.

And then I heard the words coming from that same beautiful voice that would change my life forever:

"The moment has finally arrived, Sergio, and you know it. You have two choices. To keep closing deal after deal for the rest of your life, living a life you were not supposed to live, or you can go back to your roots, to your true essence. Sometimes these moments of enlightenment come only once in a lifetime: it's in you to decide: It's now, or never.

The rest is vague. I remember Richard coming to my side, asking me if I felt okay, offering me a glass of water. My shirt was soaked with sweat.

With the little strength I had left in me, I said to Richard: "I need to get out of here. Can you please close the meeting for me?"

"Of course, he said; whatever you want. Do you want me to call a doctor?"

"No, just please close the deal and the meeting. Please! We will meet in the lobby in an hour."

"No worries Sergio. Go wash your face. You're sweating like hell!"

The rest is still blurry. I remember getting myself out of the room, and start running: running as fast as I could. People stared at me, worried. I stumbled onto a lady that worked in the hotel.

"Where can I find the Business Center?" I asked her.

"Just keep going straight and take the second left. You will see it in front of you." She stared at me. "Are you okay, Sir?"

"No, I'm not okay. But thanks."

I kept running to what it felt like an eternity until I reached the Business Center of the building. A beautiful but worried lady asked me if I needed help.

"Yes," I answered. "I need a pen, a piece of paper and a fax machine."

In no time I was sitting at one of the tables. My hands were trembling. I was shivering. I wrote some words, signed the paper and wrote a phone number. Then I went back to the lady.

"Can you fax this letter immediately to Sydney to the phone number I have written?" I asked her.

"Of course, Sir. It will only take a few seconds"

"Can I have a scotch on the rocks while I wait?"

"Sure," she said. In no time a waitress brought the glass with ice and a bottle of Blue Johnnie Walker. She started pouring the liquid into the glass.

I could hear the fax machine working, while the waitress kept filling the glass, looking at me to know when to stop.

"Keep going," I said.

Feeling worried, but saying nothing, she completely filled the glass.

"Cash or credit?" she asked.

I took a one hundred bill from my wallet. "Keep the change," I said.

In less than five minutes I had emptied my glass. The Business Center lady approached me. "Here's the confirmation that the fax went through," she said.

"Thanks," I replied. I grabbed the piece of paper, and rushed out of the Business Center. I still felt I was running out of air, but the terror I felt was starting to fade. I immediately looked for the closest elevator. Once inside, I pressed the ground floor button. It descended rapidly, but I just wanted to get out of there. I needed space!

Finally the doors opened. I ran out of the elevator, opened the crystal doors to exit the building, and sat down in a bench that overlooked the Bay of Singapore, the ocean in front of me. And I started to cry, like a seven-year old child...

I had send a fax tendering my resignation to my company headquarters.

Dear Daniel,

For some reason I still don't understand, we, human beings, start to compete against each other. We start to compare each other for the size of the house we live in, or the car we drive, even for the color of our skin, and that's when everything starts to get messed up. People who own a bigger house than their neighbors feel they are better; not all of us, but most. A doctor is definitely better than a musician, and of course at the end of the ladder is the garbage man. Suddenly you start hearing terms such as "blue collar" workers and "white collar" workers. It seems that being a "white collar" worker makes you feel superior, because you earn more money, and because you earn more money, you can buy more things, live more comfortably, have a decent education, go on holidays as you please...

Daniel, it took me exactly 34 years of my life to realize that all these issues were just lies: simply grown-up lies. And during some time through my life I felt lost; lost because in some way I was part of the minority, which believes that the real treasures of life are found in the simplest things. I truly didn't feel any pleasure in driving a better car, or wearing an expensive watch, or flying first class. I just didn't. But the system beat me for a while, and I became part of it. And sometimes I felt very lonely Daniel, surrounded by strangers that saw the world in a totally different way than I see it. Things like watching a humming bird, watching the sunset on the horizon, or staring at the dolphins jumping in the surf — those were the things that really made me happy.

I'll never forget a conversation with a friend I had during lunch at a very cozy Italian restaurant:

"You and your dolphins!" he would say "You and your surfing!" "When will you grow up?"

"What do you want to do with your life?" he asked."

I will never forget my answer, an answer that for the first time in a long time came from the bottom of my heart:

"I still don't know what I want for my life," I said. "But believe me, I know exactly what I don't want for my life."

Always try to live the life you want to live, Daniel. Believe me; it will make all the difference in the world!

From your father, who made a huge mistake in life-and rectified it.

And talking about alcohol, that whisky I drank in the Business Center of a hotel in Singapore would be the last drink I would ever have in my life.

With all the honesty in the world,

Sergio

XIV

I stayed in Singapore for the next two days. Luckily, Richard was there with me.

His first reaction, after hearing the news from me, was shock.

"What have you done?" he asked me.

"Something I should have done a long time ago," I said. "What's the point of living a life you're told to live if you feel miserable? My philosophy of what happiness in life is has nothing to do with the way I was living."

"So why did you accept the job?" he asked.

"I'm still trying to figure it out," I replied. "Maybe because ever since I was young I was taught that success meant living surrounded by beautiful material possessions, maybe because having money would take away any pain I could suffer throughout my life. Maybe it was pure greed. I really don't know"

"So what are you going to do know?'"

"Return to Australia, face the music and the peer pressure and start to live the life I always wanted to live. I'll probably take a sabbatical year off, to pull myself together again."

I returned to Sydney, and went directly to the office. Not too many smiling faces, I can say. They informed me I had to call headquarters in London, to talk with the CEO of the company.

"Hi Bill, it's Sergio..."

"Hi Sergio..."

A long silence at the other side of the telephone line…

"Are you sure about your decision?" Bill asked.

"I am."

"No regrets?"

"I hope not. I have realized that you only live once, dear Bill, so I will take the chance to live the life my heart is telling me to live. At least, if things go wrong, I won't have anyone to blame. But it's my life."

I heard Bill laughing.

"What's so funny?" I asked.

"I always knew this might happen, sooner or later," he said, "because at some stage in my life I almost made decision like the one you've already made. I just didn't think you had the balls to do it. I admire you Sergio. I have seen many people trapped in a life they hate, and yet they keep living it, afraid of the change, afraid of leaving the safety zone."

"Thanks Bill," I said.

"No, thanks to you Sergio: working with you has been great, and you have made many shareholders very happy. You've done a great job for the company, and we are grateful for that. So go on with your life. I really hope you find what you're searching for. The doors of the company will always be open for you, if you change your mind."

"Thanks Bill."

"Have a wonderful life Sergio. Bye for now."

It took me one week to clear up all the backed up paperwork. My office peers, though most of them thought I was crazy walking away, gave me a farewell party and wished me the best. I gave back my Lexus, the keys of the beautiful house I lived in, and moved to a small apartment in the Southern Beaches of Sydney, in front of the ocean. I rented it for a month.

Only then did I realize what I had done:

I had finally broken through the crystal walls for the last time, and start flying towards my dreams.

But there was still one thing I had to do. I opened the Sydney's phone directory, looked for a number, and dial it. A brief conversation went on. Finally I thanked the person at the other side of the phone line, and hanged the phone.

And that night, I went to my first A.A. meeting.

I stayed on to surf the southern beaches of Sydney for a couple of weeks.

After a while, I felt a bit afraid, and had second thoughts; because it's part of the human condition to be unsure of the decisions you take when you don't know what the future will bring. Of course I felt at peace with myself. No more planes, no more hotels, no more fancy dinners I had to attend, but most important, no more alcohol. Groups of wonderful people in A.A. groups helped me deal with the first tough months of breaking the habit. Then, using a wonderful program called "The Twelve Steps," I learned to live one day at a time. Little by little, as I grew spiritually, my craving for a drink faded away.

Now I can say that it's been many years since I had that final drink, and accepted my reality: I'm allergic to alcohol.

I feel re-born. The best days of my life are still to come: this, I know.

One day I was browsing in a bookstore in Sydney, in the sports section. A book caught my attention; "The Stormrider Surf Guide Europe." I grabbed it, and started to leaf through it. Although at this stage of my life I'd been able to circle the world and surf so many legendary spots, Europe had never been in my plans. I was amazed to see the waves that existed in Northern France, Spain and Portugal. My heart started pumping, a sign I now knew so well.

Sabbatical year? New surf spots to discover?

The decision was taken. I would travel to Europe to surf and get to know its wonderful culture for a year.

Luckily for me, I knew since I was a kid that where there's a will, there's always a way.

So I started planning my trip. What should I take? It would definitely be a backpacker's journey, but I loved my freedom, so I'd need a car — maybe even a small campervan that I could use to sleep in, with a small kitchenette and some good music. Besides that, I just required my two surfboards, a laptop to check expenses, my faithful guitar, and my dreams. I love traveling light.

I contacted a dealership in Germany, where you could rent the famous Westphalia, pay for it, use it for a year, and when you turned it in, they'd buy back the van back at a reasonable price. I also bought a cookbook. If there is a place where you can drive one or two hundred kilometers and suddenly feel you are in another world, that place was Europe. Croissants and wonderful coffee in France, tapas and good wine in Spain, pasta in beautiful Italy, Mediterranean healthy food in Greece, and the list goes on. So the decision was made. A sabbatical year throughout Europe, discovering wonderful cultures, riding some wonderful waves; slowing the pace, trying to put my life together again.

And then what?

I didn't know it at that time, but soon I would realize that if you live the life you were supposed to live, the universe will always make sure you reach a safe port.

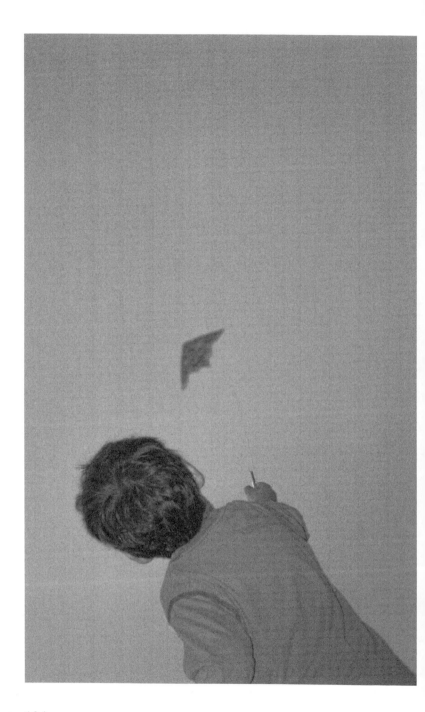

Dear Daniel,

I want to give you a present. No special occasion: special occasions, at least for me, is when you give something to others, without asking anything in return. Why wait for your birthday, or Christmas, if you can do it every day?

It's "My dream Wish towards Happiness" Daniel, and the Life I was meant to live. I hope you will be able to rescue some thoughts written in the following lines, but only if that's what you want Daniel. I just want to share with you the experience of a simple human being that never quit on his dreams:

• Always do whatever makes you feel happy. If you have to give up some of the traditions and beliefs you were taught throughout your childhood in order to feel free and be able to listen to your heart and to your dreams, do it.

• Be your own best friend. Learn that moments of solitude, far away from the bustling noise, will let you discover who you truly are. Wherever you love to be, if you are at peace with yourself surrounded by others, or just by yourself, you will have achieved something very few can: a true life, based on your own principles.

• Leave your comfort zone, get out of the box: go away. Break all the walls that you have built around you. Be free; let your spirit fly towards your destiny.

Always remember that the only treasures you will be able to take with you when your time comes to leave this world will be the memories of the dreams you achieved or at least tried your best to achieve, and the only things you will be able to leave in this world are the good or bad things you have done to turn this world into a better or worse place. Every single material possession in life is only borrowed for as long as you live on Earth, Daniel. Never forget that!

Once and for all, forget forever what others might think or say. It's your life, and as long as you respect the life of others, never worry when others speak about you. Gossip is irrelevant. It only hurts those who practice it.

The only person you should compete with in this world is with yourself, and no one else. Try to be a better person each new day, one day at a time.

The day I was able to erase words such as hate, vengeance, resentment, rivalry, and delete them from my mind's memory and from my heart, I felt like a new human being. It took me years to understand this wonderful lesson: "If someone slaps you in the face, turn the other cheek." Humility is a state of spirituality I never imagined being able to achieve, and that made the difference. Try it Daniel, it feels good!

Never forget this: a loser is not the one who doesn't achieve his goals in life, but the one that never tries. You only live once, my beloved Daniel. At least in this world.

Live!

Your friend and father,

Sergio

XV

I've been in Europe for eight months. Starting my trip from Frankfurt, in a second-hand Westphalia, I have traveled through wonderful lands, and I have discovered beautiful surfing spots along the way. I have driven more than ten thousand kilometers! I am amazed to realize that the most beautiful places in Europe, at least for me, are not part of the "must-go — tourist places in the Old Continent. Again, going the extra mile, putting "why not?" in place of "no." You can discover places you didn't even know existed, hidden jewels. Paris, London, Berlin, Rome are all wonderful cities with majestic museums, cathedrals and arts. There's no doubt about it. But in the end they're just that: cities.

And the surf! Awesome! Biarritz and Hossegor in France, the green coast of Northern Spain. The legendary waves of Mundaka, in the Basque country, even the gentle and mellow waves of places outside Tarifa, in Southern Spain. Surfers from all over the world and all ages, traveling just like me. Soul-surfers who had left everything to do what they loved the most: gliding on a moving wall of water. I felt I was back with my tribe, where I belonged, once again.

I will definitely would return to Mount Saint Mitchell in France, the Amalfi Coast in Italy, or the mountains of Assisi, the lush green forests of Northern Spain, Biarritz in France, the Romenische Strasse in Germany, places that you will remember forever.

After nine months, discovering beautiful Europe and its wonderful people, my trip was coming to an end.

My final destination was Portugal, which I had planned to visit for a week, to enjoy surfing its good waves and learn about its lovely capital, Lisbon.

I felt so in love with the place, its people and its waves that I stayed three months: that's where the real change in my life started, although I didn't know it yet. But again, the answer was in the ocean, as Lisbon is the only capital city in Western Europe washed by the ocean.

Just pure, simple coincidence?

Not at all: this I know now, but not then.

There is a beautiful camping site 15 kilometers north of Lisbon.

It's called Orbitur, and if you drive through La Marginal, a wonderful, meandering road that kisses the ocean where the raging North Atlantic surf breaks against the rocky coasts of the Portuguese coast, you will suddenly find yourself embraced by pinheiros, beautiful small pine trees that cover the land like a jungle. Right in front of the Orbitur Camping site is Guincho, a beautiful open beach that is famous worldwide for its windsurf conditions, and, to a small group of enthusiasts, for its surfing.

In the far distance, covered in lush green pinewoods, you can see the Serra de Estrelha (Mountains of the Stars). There's beautiful palace that once belonged to the Catholic kings as well as a Muslim castle. They bear silent witnesses to times gone by, when the Iberian Peninsula was conquered and re-conquered by Muslims and Christians, in the infamous times of the Crusades.

The place has its own energy, and during the day, kilometers of white sands rim the dark blue waters of the Atlantic Ocean. At night, the whistling wind sometimes blows so strong that you could swear it would turn your van over. But the caravan site is made in such a way that every site is well protected from the strong winds.

This is the place I used as a base to surf the best waves in Europe. From Peniche at the North to the beaches closer to Lisbon, like Carcavelos and Sao Pedro de Estoril, it was a surfer's dream. There was always somewhere you could surf! Depending on the size of the swell, the bigger they got, the closer to Lisbon you had to surf, as the city gets shelter from the huge Atlantic storms from the natural way the bay bends towards the south. Sometimes offshore, sometimes in totally glassy waters, without a drop of wind, I really started to remember my roots. When getting out of the water and drying myself, I could see groups of young kids arriving at the beach, all excited after school, to catch one or two waves before the last rays of the sun melted in the horizon. The same way I did with my friends in Lima, when I was the same age.

At this stage of my trip I had already decided that after going back to Australia, I'd look for a job that would allow me to work from home, probably earning less money. I wanted a job that would give me back one of my most precious treasures in life: time to live.

My stay in Portugal turned into a wonderful adventure. Surfing different spots every day, going to the market to buy my own fresh vegetables and groceries and cooking in the small kitchenette inside my faithful Westphalia, I would pull up the roof and open all doors to feel more spacious. On one of the side windows I had placed a small poster with some lines written by Confucius:

My house is very small,

but its doors and windows open

into a vast

and wonderful world

I looked at it every day, and thanked life for giving me the strength and a second opportunity to break the rules, to cross the crystal walls, and to live the life I really wanted to live.

As I said at the beginning, the only material possessions I took on my driving trip to Europe were my two surfboards, my faithful guitar and a laptop.

The reason I took a laptop with me was to control my daily expenses, and be sure that the money I had saved would last for a year.

When I left Australia, I gave everything away to charity. People thought I was crazy, but wouldn't it have been too easy to travel around Europe and then return to Australia where I knew a big bank account was awaiting me? If I really wanted to find and discover my roots, I had to start from scratch.

So I gave everything I had away, and kept only enough money to buy an old camper van, and the money to allow me to travel as a backpacker in Europe for a year, plus my return air ticket. Every night I would enter my expenses my daily expenses into my computer: petrol, food, and any other extras; that way, I could control my budget and hopefully make it last for the whole year that I had planned to stay in Europe.

But as I said before, life has hidden surprises for those who follow the voice of their hearts and follow their dreams; and it certainly had a surprise for me.

It happened one morning as I was surfing in a beautiful sunny day in Guincho. I caught a wave, and glided through the wall of water. Suddenly, a black figure emerged at my side. My first thought was "it's a shark," as the waters of the North Atlantic are normally too cold for dolphins. I left the wave and sat on my surfboard, my legs and feet out of the water.

It suddenly appeared again. It was a wonderful dolphin. He started to circle me, as if to say, "Let's play!" So I caught the next wave. In no time, the dolphin appeared in front of me, both surfing the same wave, enjoying the moment like only children know: feeling happy just for the sake of it.

Three days and two nights I surfed with this beautiful dolphin as my only companion. Surfing at night, under the full moon, is an experience I still practice until today. The brilliance of the water would tell me when some waves were approaching, and every time I caught one, this beautiful wild creature that had decided to accompany me would keep close to me, jumping behind me in the wave, suddenly re-surfacing in front of me. These moments of true joy, of feeling as alive as possible can only be compared to other crazy things I have done throughout my life, like staying in the snowcapped mountain in the Himalayas for a week, or sleeping in L"Ermita de le Carcieri, the stone and rock house built by St. Francis in the high mountains of Assisi; yes, these are moments that really touch your life so strongly that you can't help feeling happy just to be alive.

This was what I'd been yearning for. Just as one day I had to walk down from the mountains of the Himalayas to keep from freezing to death, and leave L'Ermita one step ahead of the police, the same thing happened with the wonderful dolphin: after three days and two nights of gliding together in the waves, it swam away one afternoon. It was born free to go and do as it pleased, just like me.

I was still glowing with happiness the night when I bid farewell to my wonderful surfing companion. I never saw him again. But he left me filled with energy and passion for life. The three days justified the whole year's trip: because I felt part of what was happening, and not merely a spectator-and that made all the difference.

That night, as usual, I opened my laptop. I was about to start typing in the expenses of the day.

And that's when it happened...

With the full moon glowing in the night, under the pine woods of a wonderful beach close to Lisbon, in an old-small camper van, only illuminated by the light of a computer screen and the full moon, I had a catharsis. Suddenly I felt this urge to start writing, so I did. What happened in the next three weeks of my life is something I am still trying to understand even today: for three weeks, after surfing all day, only stopping to take a nap or eat, I wrote night after night, not even looking back at what I was writing: feelings flowed from my entrails and turned into words on a computer screen.

For twenty-one nights in a row I didn't stop writing, until it was finished. I felt I had said all I needed to say. And I started crying like a child, because without noticing it, after blowing away all the dust that had covered my soul for so many years, I had finally found the key that would open the door of the golden cage I had placed myself in, and would finally be able to get out and see the world again with true eyes. And I felt free at last. The beginning of a new morning, of a new life, had finally arrived...

Dear son,

Do you want to know something that I have learned in this wonderful journey called life?

It's never too late to start again; no matter if you're ten, twenty, even 60 years old, or more: you can always be born again Daniel, spiritually speaking. There were times in my life when I felt truly lost, and I almost quit on my dreams. I was so tired of going against the flow just because I thought differently, just because I promised myself to live a life based in universal principles, and not on traditions. The going can get really tough sometimes Daniel, because there is no one out there to show you the way, to guide you to your destiny.

Only your true will, your faith in your dreams and the love of what you love the most of life makes you persevere in your endeavor. But your mind can be your best friend, or your worst enemy. It can play you tricks whenever you expect it the least, and try to force you to quit. On top of that, sometimes feeling depressed or having an addiction can really blur your mind, and make you forget what you went out to achieve: to find the true purpose of your life, by following your dreams.

But if you never forget your essence, your true self, and in my case, the vision of a five-year-old child sitting in the cliffs watching the crashing surf and listening to the salty wind whispering words straight to my heart, you will make it. Hold tight to those wonderful memories long gone Daniel: stick to the wonder of a child that thinks

115

that nothing is impossible, that you came to this world to live the life you always wanted to live. Never lose that special brightness in your eyes that comes directly from your soul. And if you lose it, always fight to recover it.

All paths in life will always be open for an open heart and an open mind: free will at its best. But I won't lie to you, beautiful Daniel: sometimes it can get really rough. Only if you persevere, stick to what you went out to achieve by following the dictates of your heart, and staying young at heart...well, you will discover what you went out to achieve, and much more...

I have many spiritual wounds and physical scars Daniel. They prove to me that I tried my best. And that's enough for me, as the human being I am.

With all my love and light, your Sergio, Daniel.

Yes, my beloved Daniel,

I finally learned the lesson, and put it in practice. The society in which I grew always told me that the road to success would be to climb the ladders of my career as fast as I could, so I could get the financial means to buy all kind of fancy material possessions, and that, somehow, by owning all these "treasures," I would be better than most human beings: more important, more respected, more happy...

In my case, money, power and arrogance threw me to a black hole from which luckily I was able to emerge. I am not saying it's bad to have these things Daniel, if that's what you want for your life. I can only talk about me, and no one else.

But I guess I have a small edge on my side: I have seen both sides of the crystal wall, Daniel; not many are lucky to experience both kind of lives: one based on your dreams and the dictates of your heart, and the other one based in financial success, living in the safe-box, filled with material possessions that take you precious time just to keep them. But maybe many people are happy living in the safe-box. If they are happy, I guess that's good for them. But I couldn't, and will never be able to live that way. Different human beings, Daniel: different goals in life. We don't have the right to judge anyone, Daniel: just ourselves.

And then there are those people that are always observing you, waiting for you to make a single mistake, so they can feel no guilt of living life the way our society tells us. The other day, after a book presentation, someone asked me:

"You talk about following your dreams, and living the life you were suppose to live. But probably now that you sell millions of books you are earning more money than you ever did!"

"True," I said. "But what you don't know, and that's the reason you are asking me a malicious question, is that more than ninety percent of my income goes to charity and philanthropic foundations. I just keep enough money to have financial peace of mind, which in my case is very little: a couple of surfboards, a small apartment with a view of the ocean, a second-hand four wheel drive that takes me to the places I love to surf or swim with dolphins and whales, and my faithful guitar and my little laptop where I can express what I feel."

Looking at the journalist straight in to his eyes, Daniel, I finally said:

"Oh! And of course dozens, maybe even hundreds of dreams and wonderful memories of places I have seen, human beings that I've met, and thousands of waves that I still surf in my heart, and in the ocean. Believe me: there is plenty of space in my heart to keep them. They don't take much space... I love traveling lightly..."

I love you so much Daniel. More than you will ever imagine.

Sergio

EPILOGUE

Today, November 9, 2009, the movie has been seen in all Latin America and Brazil. It's a hit; our Distributor for Latin America, 20th Century Fox also took all rights for North America. Our sale's agent for the rest of the world is Celluloid Dreams, which has already sold most of the rights for the movie to be screened worldwide. Three weeks ago, Fox announced that "The Dolphin, The Story of a Dreamer" had pre-qualified to compete with another twenty animated movies from all over the world for the Academy Awards in the category "Best Animated Featured Film for 2009"

We are in the race for an Oscar.

The next time that I hear the word impossible, it will be as someone is talking to me in a different language that I don't understand: passion for what you do, faith, hard work and perseverance is all you need. The rest will naturally flow.

I just came out of the cinema. It's a Sunday evening; to be more exact December 1, 2009, and I went see "The Dolphin." It is my birthday. Forty-nine years old. Unbelievable how time flies! Nonetheless, it doesn't worry me at all.

The reason I went to see the film we created was that today would probably be the last day to be able to see it on the big screen in Latin America. Humbly speaking, the theatre was packed. And yet, watching so many children laugh and have a good time, and many adults, maybe not laughing so strongly, but definitely paying attention to some scenes that are directed to them, I can see that we achieved what we wanted — to touch a string in their hearts. Who knows? Maybe when they leave the cinema they will think about their lives. Maybe we will have been able to open a small window in their hearts, and help them realize that there are many ways to live a life, and maybe most important of all, to live the life you were meant to live. I can see in their eyes the doubts, feeling a bit uncomfortable for what they have just seen and heard: and that's exactly what we wanted to do.

Twentieth Century Fox is very happy working with our small company, officially known as Dolphin Films, (but for those who work in our company better known as the "Dreamer's Club"). They have the first option to distribute worldwide the sequel of the film.

We have finally arrived to safe port after more than three years of hard work.

But for me, what makes me feel happy if having shared something with others, without asking anything in return: the best present one will ever be able to get...

Yes, my beloved Son.

Nothing is impossible, if you choose to live that way. Never lose that smile with which you wake up every morning. Never lose that deep look in your eyes that comes straight from your soul. Whatever you want to do with your life, your mother and I will be there for you, in the good and bad times. And when the time comes for you to fly with your own wings, we will be there to say good-bye, and you will always know that you will have a nest where you can always return.

But I cannot lie to you, Daniel. I have seen you watch the ocean, sometimes for hours, the way I have always done. I see how you enjoy at the simple things of life. If that's what you want, that's what you'll get. You just need to cross the crystal walls — never forget that. Beware of the way you see the world, because the world will be exactly as you see it. Summer is arriving. Your mother wants to put you in swimming classes; let's see if you like the feeling.

And who knows? Maybe one day you will want to glide in a wall of water, and follow your dreams. I hope life gives me the chance to see you grow happy, in peace. I will try to help you by teaching you principles, and that if you truly want something in life, it takes courage, persistence and faith to accomplish what you went out to achieve.

Yet, of all the tools I will give you to try to help you make your life a song of joy, this little book is the best present I will ever be able to give you: 49 years of experience in the journey through my unique life; the good and the bad.

I hope you will always treat it like your empty baby shampoo bottle you treasure so much. Because the day that you read this book, you will find the story of a simple human being that never quit on his dreams: a simple human being that made many mistakes in his life, and learnt from them. If I could do it, anyone can. .

And I can certainly tell you this, beautiful Daniel:

No regrets Daniel; not a single one.

With all my love, Daniel;

wherever you are and wherever I am.

Sergio

ABOUT THE AUTHOR

Sergio Bambaren was born the first day of December of 1960 in Lima, Peru.

Educated in a British High School, Sergio has been captivated from his early years by the ocean, having been born in a city that meets the sea. This would influence him for the rest of his life, and put him in a journey he would have never expected: to become a writer.

His adventurous spirit took him to the United States, where he graduated as a Chemical Engineer from Texas A&M University. However, the ocean was still his greatest love, and traveling gave him the opportunity to go surfing to places such as California, Hawaii, Mexico, Chile, and Central America.

After a brief stay in the country in which he was born, Sergio decided to immigrate to Sydney, Australia, where he worked as a Sales Manager for a multinational company. However, he also managed to travel to the Southeast Asia and the African coasts in search of the perfect wave. Legendary places like Bali; Nias, Jeffrey's Bay, Agadir in Morocco and the Philippines, as well as Australia and New Zeeland were part of his surfing travels.

After several years in Australia, Sergio took a sabbatical and traveled to Europe in search of the perfect wave. It was in Portugal, at a wonderful beach surrounded by pine forests called Guincho, that Sergio found the purpose of his life and a very special friend: a dolphin that inspired him to write *The Dolphin: Story of a Dreamer.*

After he returned to Sydney, Sergio self-published his book in Oz. this happened in 1996. Suddenly, everything changed in Sergio's life. He sold more than 100,000 copies of "The Dolphin" in Australia in less than a year.

The Dolphin has now been translated into 40 languages and dialects. The book has appeared on bestseller lists in Germany, France, Italy, Latin America, and elsewhere. The story has also been adapted for an animated movie called The Dreaming Dolphin.

Sergio's subsequent novels, including Beach of Dreams, Distant Winds, The Guardian of the Light, The Story of Iris, Tales from the Heavens, Thoughts by the Ocean, and Angels of the Sea have also become extremely popular and have been published in more than seventy countries.

Follow your dreams. Listen to your heart.

Whatever others might tell you,

never forget that you only live once

and that your dreams, big or small,

are the greatest treasures that will guide your life

to a unique and wonderful destiny.

Don't let your fears

stand in the way of your dreams.

Printed in Great
Britain
by Amazon